RUSSIAN AND CHINESE NUCLEAR ARSENALS: POSTURE, PROLIFERATION, AND THE FUTURE OF ARMS CONTROL

HEARING

BEFORE THE

SUBCOMMITTEE ON TERRORISM, NONPROLIFERATION, AND TRADE

OF THE

COMMITTEE ON FOREIGN AFFAIRS HOUSE OF REPRESENTATIVES

ONE HUNDRED FIFTEENTH CONGRESS

SECOND SESSION

JUNE 21, 2018

Serial No. 115–141

Printed for the use of the Committee on Foreign Affairs

Available: http://www.foreignaffairs.house.gov/, http://docs.house.gov, or http://www.gpo.gov/fdsys/

U.S. GOVERNMENT PUBLISHING OFFICE

WASHINGTON : 2018

30–499PDF

COMMITTEE ON FOREIGN AFFAIRS

EDWARD R. ROYCE, California, *Chairman*

CHRISTOPHER H. SMITH, New Jersey
ILEANA ROS-LEHTINEN, Florida
DANA ROHRABACHER, California
STEVE CHABOT, Ohio
JOE WILSON, South Carolina
MICHAEL T. McCAUL, Texas
TED POE, Texas
DARRELL E. ISSA, California
TOM MARINO, Pennsylvania
MO BROOKS, Alabama PAUL
COOK, California SCOTT
PERRY, Pennsylvania RON
DeSANTIS, Florida
MARK MEADOWS, North Carolina
TED S. YOHO, Florida
ADAM KINZINGER, Illinois
LEE M. ZELDIN, New York
DANIEL M. DONOVAN, JR., New York
F. JAMES SENSENBRENNER, JR.,
  Wisconsin
ANN WAGNER, Missouri
BRIAN J. MAST, Florida
FRANCIS ROONEY, Florida
BRIAN K. FITZPATRICK, Pennsylvania
THOMAS A. GARRETT, JR., Virginia
JOHN R. CURTIS, Utah

ELIOT L. ENGEL, New York
BRAD SHERMAN, California
GREGORY W. MEEKS, New York
ALBIO SIRES, New Jersey
GERALD E. CONNOLLY, Virginia
THEODORE E. DEUTCH, Florida
KAREN BASS, California
WILLIAM R. KEATING, Massachusetts
DAVID N. CICILLINE, Rhode Island
AMI BERA, California
LOIS FRANKEL, Florida
TULSI GABBARD, Hawaii
JOAQUIN CASTRO, Texas
ROBIN L. KELLY, Illinois
BRENDAN F. BOYLE, Pennsylvania
DINA TITUS, Nevada
NORMA J. TORRES, California
BRADLEY SCOTT SCHNEIDER, Illinois
THOMAS R. SUOZZI, New York
ADRIANO ESPAILLAT, New York
TED LIEU, California

AMY PORTER, *Chief of Staff*   THOMAS SHEEHY, *Staff Director*
JASON STEINBAUM, *Democratic Staff Director*

––––––

SUBCOMMITTEE ON TERRORISM, NONPROLIFERATION, AND TRADE

TED POE, Texas, *Chairman*

JOE WILSON, South Carolina
DARRELL E. ISSA, California
PAUL COOK, California
SCOTT PERRY, Pennsylvania
LEE M. ZELDIN, New York
BRIAN J. MAST, Florida
THOMAS A. GARRETT, JR., Virginia

WILLIAM R. KEATING, Massachusetts
LOIS FRANKEL, Florida
BRENDAN F. BOYLE, Pennsylvania
DINA TITUS, Nevada
NORMA J. TORRES, California
BRADLEY SCOTT SCHNEIDER, Illinois

CONTENTS

RUSSIAN AND CHINESE NUCLEAR ARSENALS: POSTURE, PROLIFERATION, AND THE FUTURE OF ARMS CONTROL

THURSDAY, JUNE 21, 2018

House of Representatives,
Subcommittee on Terrorism, Nonproliferation, and Trade,
Committee on Foreign Affairs,
Washington, DC.

The subcommittee met, pursuant to notice, at 2:00 p.m., in room 2172 Rayburn House Office Building, Hon. Ted Poe (chairman of the subcommittee) presiding.

Mr. POE. The subcommittee will come to order. Without objection, all members may have 5 days to submit statements, questions, and extraneous materials for the record and subject to length limitation in the rules. The Chair will dispense with my opening statement and I will file it as part of the record. I will yield to the ranking member, Mr. Keating, from Massachusetts.

[The prepared statement of Mr. Poe follows:]

Congressman Ted Poe
Statement for the Record
TNT Hearing, "Russian and Chinese Nuclear Arsenals: Posture, Proliferation, and the Future of Arms Control"

The world today is in a new era of great power rivalry. Resurgent Russia and China are challenging U.S. interests across the globe. Both are rapidly modernizing their militaries to directly challenge America's dominance on the battlefield and to undermine our alliances around the world. The potential for major conflict is closer now than it has been since the Cold War.

China and Russia's rising power has huge implications for how we trade, how we target rogue regimes, and how the entire international system works. While we often focus on Iran and North Korea's nuclear programs, we tend to overlook the two atomic arsenals that pose the greatest danger to our security. But with Russia and China's aggressive behavior in places like Ukraine, Georgia, and the South China Sea, we are forced to rethink our deterrence against such threats.

Comparing our nuclear arsenals, it's clear China and Russia have been intent on challenging U.S. dominance and coercing our friends for some time. While we have barely upgraded some of our nuclear systems since they were first deployed in the early 1980s, China and Russia have introduced new weapons. We may be reluctant to maintain and upgrade such devastating weapons, but our strategic rivals are not. If we allow Russia or China to achieve nuclear superiority over us, the results will be dire for our allies and for the international order we have spent decades building.

Just in March, Vladimir Putin unveiled several new nuclear weapons intended to make our missile defenses "useless." They include a new heavy ICBM, a nuclear-powered cruise missile with "unlimited range," and a nuclear- powered unmanned submarine designed to sneak into coastal cities and explode. Such a heavy investment in nuclear arms is concerning and demonstrates Putin's priority is not disarmament but strategic dominance.

However, Putin left something out of his threatening display. He did not include the new ground-launched cruise missile which the State Department has said for years is violating the INF Treaty. This missile undermines years of arms control negotiations and the good faith we have hoped to build with the Russians since the end of the Cold War. With the New START treaty expiring in 2021, the INF violation casts real doubt on continued strategic arms limitations with the Russians going forward. If the START treaty expires, the Russians will be completely free to expand their nuclear stockpile to what it was during the darkest days of the Cold War. This will likely force others—including ourselves—to also build more bombs.

Worse, now that China is a major rival, we could be pushed into a situation more dangerous than the Cold War. We have been fortunate that China has kept its nuclear stockpile relatively small, focusing on minimal deterrence. But China is building new delivery systems to match our own and is not restrained to arms control agreements like those between the U.S. and Russia. China is rapidly building new ballistic missile submarines and mobile ICBMs which will further strain our military's ability to track. Beijing is also making advances in hypersonic missiles that will make early warning systems ineffective.

Yet, the major concern with China is its willingness to proliferate nuclear technology to rogue regimes. Iran, North Korea, and Pakistan have all benefited from Chinese assistance. In many cases, China has directly sold nuclear and missile technology to these terrorist regimes. China's low regard for non-proliferation standards has been irresponsible and created increased instability around the globe.

For too long we have not address the source of these rising threats. North Korea and Iran are major problems, but they would be far more isolated and far less dangerous if they did not have backing from Russia and China. Even our need for missile defense—which China and Russia claim is so destabilizing—would be unnecessary if these rogue regimes did not have help from Moscow and Beijing.

As we think about the future of our nuclear forces and the future of arms control, we must have a clear view of the threats we face. China and Russia are capable adversaries. Left unchecked they will surpass us and make the world less safe. Therefore, we must continue to engage them to restrict the number and capability of these terrible weapons while making clear we will not allow them to gain the nuclear advantage.

Ronald Reagan once said, "a nuclear war cannot be won and must never be fought." We must continue his legacy by seeking a world without nuclear arms. And that's just the way it is.

Mr. KEATING. Thank you, Mr. Chairman. I will also submit my opening statement for the record because of the delay and it occurs on the rollcall, and I will yield back to you. I thank our witnesses for being here, particularly Mr. Rose who once lived in America's hometown: Plymouth, Massachusetts. I yield back.

[The prepared statement of Mr. Keating follows:]

Congressman William Keating
Statement for the Record
TNT Hearing, "Russian and Chinese Nuclear Arsenals: Posture, Proliferation, and the Future of Arms Control"

I'd like to thank the Chairman for convening this hearing today. We're meeting today on Russian and Chinese nuclear arsenals and in particular, in the context of the future of arms control.

I think it's helpful and important to step back for a moment and reflect on the global context for arms control. I believe it's fair to say that North Korea and Iran are the countries that come to mind when someone raises the issue of nuclear weapons and arms control. We have faced grave security threats from Iranian and North Korean nuclear ambitions and have had to work very hard to manage these threats and strive towards greater peace and stability in our time.

With Iran, the U.S. worked closely with our allies to negotiate a framework and agreement for bringing Iran back into the fold on compliance with international norms and practices. There was accountability in that agreement, and it's hard to deny that we have been safer with that agreement than without it.

Nuclear weapons – and the many strategic capabilities that go along with maintaining a nuclear arsenal – present some of the most challenging geopolitical, security, and frankly existential questions that we as a country and other countries around the world must answer. We have to answer these questions for ourselves, however, we must also negotiate this sensitive terrain alongside other countries that are not always in lockstep with our vision for what a peaceful and stable arms control regime should look like.

That brings us to the topic at hand today: Russian and Chinese nuclear arsenals. U.S. efforts with Russia have not always been met with resounding success. We are regularly at odds with one another on the extent to which we believe international laws and norms must be respected. That's just a fact of our relationship, but it does not have to be the end of the story. While we dislike – or even at times, condemn – Putin's actions and violations of our arms control and other agreements, that does not mean our hands are tied in continuing to promote global nonproliferation commitments and efforts to hold Russia and others accountable to them. We also cannot afford to pivot away from China on these issues. The development of their own nuclear arsenal and more advanced capabilities in space and in cyber, demand that we take engagement with China on these issues seriously.

U.S. leadership on these issues is a matter of our own immediate and long-term security, but also of our ability to shape an international order based on rules, commitments, and checks. This order gives the U.S. greater security, but it also gives governments and their people around the world, the peace of mind to pursue critical objectives in economic growth, security, and in other arenas.

The threat of nuclear war or even just missteps on these issues are too great; we must be vigilant in pursuing more predictability, accountability, and stability for nuclear arms control. The U.S.

has negotiated nuclear arms control agreements in the past. We have brought together our State Department, Defense Department and national security experts alongside our closest allies to raise the standards on arms control. Our allies share our nuclear proliferation concerns and our goals for a world in which all countries abide by established norms and rules to prevent the devastation that nuclear weapons can bring. If we are going to be successful in our nonproliferation efforts with Russia and China, we have to be at our best and capitalize on our greatest strengths.

This has often been raised in this committee, but we cannot afford to continue with a weakened State Department where morale is down, where key positions remain unfilled, and where our foreign service officers and diplomats abroad do not have the full force and support of their own government behind them.

We must also modernize our own arsenal in the most strategic and impactful way that reflects the complex dynamics and threat environments we face. And we cannot allow our alliances to be weakened. We rely on our friends and allies for our own strategic defense. The nature of nuclear weapons means that we cannot go it alone no matter how great we are. Our alliances make us stronger and it will be a dangerous mistake to forget that even for a moment.

Yes, we have faced setbacks in our arms control agreements with Russia and otherwise. Negotiating arms control frameworks and agreements is a process that takes time and dedication to the objectives at hand. However, we can operate from a position of strength when it comes to Russia or China on the other side of the negotiating table.

So I am looking forward to our hearing today and to the testimony of our witnesses so that we can better evaluate how to best tackle these questions before us around arms control and the unique geopolitical challenges presented by Russia and China. I believe there are steps we can take but it does require resolve to get there. Thank you and I yield back.

Mr. POE. Without objection, the witnesses' prepared statements will be made part of the record, and I will ask that each witness keep their presentation to no more than 5 minutes. I will introduce each witness and then give them time for their opening statement.

The first witness, Dr. Austin Long, is a senior political scientist at the Rand Corporation. Previously, he was an associate professor at Columbia University's School of International and Public Affairs.

Dr. Patricia Kim is the Stanton Nuclear Security Fellow at the Council on Foreign Relations. She was previously a fellow at the Princeton-Harvard China and the World Program at the Woodrow Wilson School of Public and International Affairs.

And Mr. Frank Rose from Plymouth, Massachusetts is senior fellow for Security and Strategy in the Foreign Policy Program at the Brookings Institution. Previously he has served as assistant secretary of state for Arms Control, Verification, and Compliance.

Welcome to all three of the witnesses here. Each of you are limited to 5 minutes. Your statements are part of the record, so when you see the red light come on before you, that means to stop.

So we will start with Dr. Long. You may make your opening statement.

STATEMENT OF AUSTIN LONG, PH.D., SENIOR POLITICAL SCIENTIST, RAND CORPORATION

Mr. LONG. Chairman Poe, Ranking Member Keating, and members of the subcommittee, thank you for inviting me to address the important concerns about Russia's nuclear posture and the future of arms control. I will briefly summarize key developments in Russian nuclear forces as well as some of the factors driving those developments. I will then discuss the implications of Russian nuclear developments for the future of arms control.

Russia is modernizing almost every part of its nuclear arsenal including short-range systems, intercontinental ballistic missiles, submarine launch missiles, and air launch cruise missiles. I provide more detail on Russian modernization in my written testimony, but three developments stand out.

First, President Vladimir Putin announced in March that Russia has invested in two novel, strategic nuclear delivery systems. The first is a long-range nuclear-powered and nuclear-armed autonomous underwater vehicle. The second is an intercontinental range, nuclear-powered and nuclear-armed cruise missile. In addition, the U.S. Government in 2014 declared Russia to be testing and subsequently deploying an intermediate range ground launch cruise missile in violation of the intermediate nuclear forces or INF Treaty.

Russian nuclear development is driven in large part by fear that the combination of U.S. nuclear, conventional, and missile defense capabilities could greatly reduce the effectiveness of Russian deterrence based on nuclear retaliation. These fears date back to the Cold War but were amplified following the U.S. withdrawal from the Anti-Ballistic Missile Treaty in 2002.

Russia's fears, justified or not, could potentially precipitate a nuclear crisis between the United States and Russia. Russian leaders could perceive unrest or revolution in one of its neighbors as engineered by the United States and take what they believe to be appropriate defensive measures. U.S. and NATO leaders could take what from their perspective are equally defensive measures resulting in a crisis and possible conflict.

Moreover, if conflict did happen, Russian military commanders might recommend limited nuclear use if Russia's non-nuclear capabilities fail to terminate the conflict promptly. Whether Russian political leaders would accept such a recommendation is unknowable, but this scenario underscores that even if Russian intentions are largely defensive, nuclear crisis and limited nuclear use are possible.

This scenario also highlights the importance of arms control, yet prospects for arms control are grim. Russia denies it is violating the INF Treaty, instead leveling counter accusations against the United States with no progress on this deadlock since 2014. In contrast, both sides agree they are broadly in compliance with START, the new Strategic Arms Limitation Treaty or New START. New START expires in 2021, although there is an option to extend it for 5 years if both parties agree. However, dialogue appears frozen at present as I discuss in more detail in written testimony.

From the U.S. perspective as embodied in the 2018 Nuclear Posture Review, Russia is an unrepentant violator of existing arms control agreements. From the Russian perspective, the United States has been neutralizing Russia's strategic deterrent and destroying the Russian state. Given these divergent views, the instinct may be to simply walk away from arms control.

While this is understandable, arms control can provide transparency and communication that help prevent nuclear crisis scenarios like the one described previously. For example, even as U.S.-Russia relations have grown tense, under New START both sides have conducted more than a 130 onsite inspections while exchanging data thousands of times. The most comprehensive solution may be to start from scratch with a broader set of negotiations on new, mutually acceptable limits for intermediate range systems, the new Russian systems, and missile defenses. Yet, the United States is reluctant to limit missile defenses against North Korea and Iran even if it does not seek to neutralize Russia's strategic deterrent as the Kremlin fears. Such a solution will also likely take a very long time to negotiate.

Absent such a comprehensive solution, it seems unlikely the Russian Government will change its behavior. The United States will thus be faced with a stark choice by 2021: Maintain New START despite Russian arms control violations or allow New START to expire and possibly withdraw from the INF Treaty as well. Maintaining New START will preserve valuable transparency, yet may confirm to the Russians that the United States treats each arms control issue separately. This could encourage further violations of INF and other treaties.

Allowing New START to expire would demonstrate that arms control violations have real consequences, yet it would mean for the first time in more than three decades that U.S.-Russian nuclear competition would be unrestrained. Perhaps a key indicator for the future would be how the Russians seek to present the novel systems Putin revealed in March. New START includes a provision on novel systems, so if the Russians are willing to address these systems for potential inclusion in New START limitations as President

Putin has, himself, publicly suggested, then extension may make sense despite Russian violation of INF and other treaties.

If the Russians are unwilling to engage in productive, official dialogue on these novel systems, it is hard to see a future for New START or, indeed, arms control generally. Thank you for your time, and I look forward to your questions.

[The prepared statement of Mr. Long follows:]

Russian Nuclear Forces and Prospects for Arms Control

Austin Long

CT-495

Testimony presented before the House of Representatives Committee on Foreign Affairs, Subcommittee on Terrorism, Nonproliferation, and Trade on June 21, 2018.

For more information on this publication, visit www.rand.org/pubs/testimonies/CT495.html

Testimonies

RAND testimonies record testimony presented or submitted by RAND associates to federal, state, or local legislative committees; government-appointed commissions and panels; and private review and oversight bodies.

Russian Nuclear Forces and Prospects for Arms Control

Testimony of Austin Long[1]
The RAND Corporation[2]

Before the Committee on Foreign Affairs
Subcommittee on Terrorism, Nonproliferation, and Trade
United States House of Representatives

June 21, 2018

In the eight years between the Obama and Trump Administrations' Nuclear Posture Reviews (NPRs), U.S.-Russia relations have grown increasingly confrontational, as vividly demonstrated in the arenas of nuclear forces and arms control. Two events underscore how dramatically relations have worsened. In April 2010, then–Presidents Dmitri Medvedev and Barack Obama signed the New Strategic Arms Reduction Treaty (New START) to much fanfare. In contrast, in March 2018, Medvedev's successor (and predecessor), Vladimir Putin, revealed two new Russian strategic nuclear delivery systems not covered in the text of New START.

In this statement, I draw upon unclassified sources to summarize developments in Russian nuclear forces and strategy over the past eight years as well as some of the factors driving those developments. I will then discuss the implications of Russian nuclear developments for arms control.

What Has Happened with Russia's Nuclear Weapons?

Since the signing of New START, Russia has continued modernizing much of its nuclear arsenal, as succinctly described in the 2018 U.S. NPR.[3] Russia's Strategic Rocket Forces have deployed a new intercontinental ballistic missile (ICBM), the SS-27 Mod 2, which can be mobile

---

[1] The opinions and conclusions expressed in this testimony are the author's alone and should not be interpreted as representing those of the RAND Corporation or any of the sponsors of its research.

[2] The RAND Corporation is a research organization that develops solutions to public policy challenges to help make communities throughout the world safer and more secure, healthier and more prosperous. RAND is nonprofit, nonpartisan, and committed to the public interest.

[3] U.S. Department of Defense, *Nuclear Posture Review*, Washington, D.C., 2018, p. 8.

or silo-based.[4] It has also continued development of the SS-X-30 heavy ICBM and has begun or extended development of two other ICBMs.[5]

The Russian Navy has deployed a new submarine-launched ballistic missile (SLBM), the SS-N-32, and a new submarine-launched cruise missile, the SS-N-30A.[6] The latter system can deliver conventional and possibly nuclear warheads; the conventionally armed version has been used in Syria. In addition to new nuclear delivery systems, the navy has deployed two new nuclear-powered submarines, the *Borei*-class ballistic missile submarine and the *Yasen*-class attack submarine; the latter can carry the SS-N-30. The Russian Aerospace Forces have deployed a new long-range nuclear cruise missile, the Kh-102, and a conventional variant, the KH-101, and have begun development of a new medium-range missile that is likely to be nuclear capable.[7]

As Putin announced in March, Russia also has invested in two novel strategic nuclear delivery systems. The first is an extremely long-range nuclear-powered and nuclear-armed autonomous underwater vehicle, known as the Status-6 or Poseidon system.[8] This system is capable of striking coastal cities or other targets from transoceanic ranges. The second is an intercontinental-range nuclear-powered and nuclear-armed cruise missile, which could hold at risk much, if not all, of the United States.[9]

Russia also continues to deploy shorter-range nuclear-capable delivery systems. In addition to the SS-26 short range missile system, which is deployed in parts of Russia that border the territory of the North Atlantic Treaty Organization (NATO), the U.S. government in 2014 declared Russia to be testing an intermediate-range ground-launched cruise missile in violation

---

[4] U.S. National Air and Space Intelligence Center, *Ballistic and Cruise Missile Threat*, Wright-Patterson Air Force Base, Ohio, 2017, p. 26. The SS-27 Mod 2 carries multiple independently targetable warheads and is known in Russia as the RS-24 Yars.

[5] U.S. National Air and Space Intelligence Center, 2017, p. 29. The SS-X-30 is known in Russia as the RS-28 Sarmat.

[6] U.S. National Air and Space Intelligence Center, 2017, pp. 30 and 37; and U.S. Department of Defense, 2018, p. 8. The SS-N-32 is known in Russia as the RSM-56 Bulava, and the SS-N-30A is known as the 3M-14 Kalibr or Biryuza.

[7] U.S. National Air and Space Intelligence Center, 2017, p. 30.

[8] Sputnik News, "'Doomsday Machine': Russia's New Weapon Reportedly Gets Nuclear Warhead (VIDEO)," webpage, May 17, 2018. As of June 18, 2018: https://sputniknews.com/russia/201805171064549993-russia-poseidon-system-torpedo/

[9] Defence Blog, "New Russian Intercontinental Cruise Missile May Endanger US National Interests," webpage, March 25, 2018. As of June 18, 2018: http://defence-blog.com/news/new-russian-intercontinental-cruise-missile-may-endanger-us-national-interests.html. The missile has been named *Burevestnik* (literally "messenger of the storm").

of the Intermediate-Range Nuclear Forces (INF) Treaty.[10] The United States subsequently claimed that Russia was deploying this missile, known as the SSC-8.[11]

While Russia and the United States are both engaged in nuclear modernization—as their respective arsenals still rely on systems built during the Cold War—Russia's modernization is much further along. Russia is also expanding its arsenal to include new systems, such as the two novel delivery systems Putin revealed in March and the alleged INF-violating SSC-8. In contrast, U.S. nuclear modernization concentrates on replacement, rather than expansion.[12] The next section addresses how Russian leaders might think about using this diverse and modernizing arsenal.

What is Russian Nuclear Strategy?

Over the past several years, and especially since the release of the 2018 NPR, the nature of Russian nuclear strategy has been a topic of intense debate. On one side of the debate is a view that characterizes Russian nuclear strategy as willing, perhaps even eager, to use the threat of limited nuclear escalation for purposes of coercion. The NPR states

> Russian strategy and doctrine emphasize the potential coercive and military uses of nuclear weapons. It mistakenly assesses that the threat of nuclear escalation or actual first use of nuclear weapons would serve to "de-escalate" a conflict on terms favorable to Russia.[13]

Proponents of this view highlight certain aspects of Russia's professional military debates on nuclear weapons as well as Russian nuclear activities (including exercises) and messages during and after the 2014 Russian occupation of Crimea.[14] This view is sometimes referred to by the shorthand expression "escalate to de-escalate" or "escalate to win."

---

[10] U.S. Department of State, *Adherence to and Compliance With Arms Control, Nonproliferation, and Disarmament Agreements and Commitments*, Washington, D.C., July 31, 2014. As of June 18, 2018: https://www.state.gov/t/avc/rls/rpt/2014/230047.htm

[11] MissileThreat CSIS Missile Defense Project, "US Official Identifies Missile Believed to Violate INF Treaty," webpage, December 8, 2017. As of June 18, 2018: https://missilethreat.csis.org/us-official-identifies-missile-believed-violate-inf-treaty/. The United States claims that the Russians designate this missile the Novator 9M729.

[12] The U.S. modernization includes a gravity bomb, the B61-12, which will eventually replace multiple types of gravity bomb; the Ground-Based Strategic Deterrent, which will replace the Minuteman ICBM; the *Columbia*-class submarine, which will replace the *Ohio*-class submarine; the Long-Range Stand-Off weapon, which will replace the AGM-86 air-launched cruise missile; the replacement for the Trident D5 missile; and the B-21 Raider heavy bomber, which will replace the B-2 Spirit. The 2018 NPR also calls for supplemental nuclear capabilities, one of which (a new sea-launched cruise missile) might constitute expansion of the U.S. arsenal. See U.S. Department of Defense, 2018, p. xii.

[13] U.S. Department of Defense, 2018, p. 8.

[14] See Brad Roberts, *The Case for U.S. Nuclear Weapons in the 21st Century*, Stanford, Calif.: Stanford University Press, 2016; David Johnson, *Russia's Conventional Precision Strike Capabilities, Regional Crises, and Nuclear Thresholds*, Livermore, Calif.: Lawrence Livermore National Laboratory Center for Global Security Research, 2018; Jacek Durkalec, "Nuclear-Backed 'Little Green Men:' Nuclear Messaging in the Ukraine Crisis," Warsaw: Polish Institute of International Affairs, 2015; and Katarzyna Zisk, "Escalation and Nuclear Weapons in Russia's Military Strategy," *The RUSI Journal*, May 2018.

The other view in the debate is that, while Russia remains serious about its nuclear arsenal, it has not substantially embraced a broadened coercive role for nuclear weapons. Analysts embracing this view argue that neither Russian doctrine nor exercises indicate that "escalate to de-escalate" is in fact a policy, and point to the Russian declaratory nuclear policy that nuclear weapons are intended to ensure the survival of the Russian state (and perhaps, depending on one's interpretation, the Putin regime).[15] Russia's major investments in non-nuclear forces is cited as supporting evidence for this view.

My own view of Russian nuclear strategy falls between these two perspectives.[16] Whatever the Russian military believes, senior Russian political leadership has been circumspect in describing the role of nuclear weapons in its strategy. While some Kremlin leaders have described nuclear strategy in expansive terms, Putin has been more reserved, noting in 2015: "We proceed from the assumption that nuclear weapons and other weapons are the means to protect our sovereignty and legitimate interests, not the means to behave aggressively or to fulfil some nonexistent imperial ambitions."[17]

This statement by Putin accords with Russian behavior. Whatever Russia's signaling with nuclear weapons was over Crimea, Putin and the rest of Russia's leadership clearly believed this situation was crucial to Russian security. Yet in other important but less crucial situations, Russia did not brandish the threat of nuclear weapons. For example, Russia did not invoke nuclear weapons following Turkey's downing of a Russian fighter in November 2015.[18]

Russian behavior, along with Russian acquisition of substantial non-nuclear capabilities, including long-range precision strike, offensive cyber, and counterspace systems, suggest Russian leaders are preparing for a variety of military options short of a massive nuclear exchange.[19] These options would include limited nuclear use in dire circumstances. Yet dire circumstances, from a Russian perspective, could occur very quickly in a conflict, as discussed in the next section.

---

[15] See Olga Oliker and Andrey Baklitsky, "The Nuclear Posture Review and Russian 'De-escalation:' A Dangerous Solution to a Non-Existent Problem," *War on the Rocks*, February 20, 2018. As of June 18, 2018: https://warontherocks.com/2018/02/nuclear-posture-review-russian-de-escalation-dangerous-solution-nonexistent-problem; and Bruno Tertrais, "Russia's Nuclear Policy: Worrying for the Wrong Reasons," *Survival*, Vol. 60, No. 2, March–April 2018.

[16] For a more detailed discussion, see Austin Long, "Nuclear Strategy in an Era of Great Power Competition," *Texas National Security Review* Policy Roundtable, February 13, 2018a. As of June 18, 2018: https://tnsr.org/roundtable/policy-roundtable-trump-administrations-nuclear-posture-review/#essay3

[17] CBS Sixty Minutes. "All Eyes on Putin," webpage, September 27, 2015. As of June 18, 2018: https://www.cbsnews.com/news/vladimir-putin-russian-president-60-minutes-charlie-rose/

[18] Neil MacFarquhar, "Navigator of Downed Russian Plane Says There Was No Warning," *New York Times*, November 25, 2015. As of June 18, 2018: https://www.nytimes.com/2015/11/26/world/europe/turkey-russia-jet.html

[19] See similar arguments in Kristin ven Bruusgaard, "Russian Strategic Deterrence," *Survival*, Vol. 58, No. 4, August–September 2016. and Dmitri (Dima) Adamsky, "From Moscow with Coercion: Russian Deterrence Theory and Strategic Culture," *Journal of Strategic Studies*, Vol 41, No. 1-2, January-February 2018.

What Factors Are Driving Russian Nuclear Developments?

Russian nuclear strategy and forces have been developed to meet the challenges Russian leaders have identified in their security environment. The major challenges, which have their roots in the Cold War, are the United States and NATO, with China being an important but secondary challenge. Russian leaders perceive the United States as untrustworthy at a minimum, dating back to broken promises over NATO expansion, and as actively seeking to undermine the Russian government.[20]

Russian leaders have also greatly feared U.S. nuclear and missile defense capabilities since the Cold War. The Soviets were fearful that the combination of those capabilities could greatly reduce the effectiveness of a Soviet strike on the United States, undermining Soviet deterrence. In the 1970s, this fear led the Soviets to sign the Anti-Ballistic Missile (ABM) Treaty as well as accept the limits on the quantity of nuclear forces in the Strategic Arms Limitation Talks (SALT).[21]

Yet by the early 1980s, Soviet leaders were confronted with a growing qualitative improvement in U.S. nuclear forces and the prospect of the United States leaving the ABM Treaty with the announcement of the Strategic Defense Initiative (SDI, aka "Star Wars"). Soviet assessments became deeply pessimistic, with some indicating that by the mid-1990s, the Soviets might only be able to strike 100 targets in retaliation following a U.S. first strike.[22] If U.S. missile defenses were even modestly effective, that number might be reduced by half, while highly effective defenses might reduce that number to ten or perhaps even zero.

Russian leaders have inherited these Soviet fears from the 1980s, which were amplified following the U.S. withdrawal from the ABM Treaty in 2002. The developments over the past eight years in Russian nuclear strategy and forces have been an attempt to address these fears. Perhaps unsurprisingly, the two novel delivery systems Putin announced in March appear to have originated in the late Soviet period as means to circumvent SDI.[23]

Yet in addition to fears from the Soviet era, Russian leaders have two new fears. The first is the "precision revolution" in conventional munitions, which Russia has observed closely since the Gulf War in 1991. Based on these observations, the Russians now believe a massive first-strike volley of conventional precision munitions could be effective in neutralizing much of their strategic deterrent or crippling the government, highlighting U.S. "shock and awe"-style

---

[20] Joshua Itzkowitz Shifrinson, "Deal or No Deal? The End of the Cold War and the U.S. Offer to Limit NATO Expansion," *International Security*, Vol. 46, No. 4, Spring 2016.

[21] For a more detailed discussion, see Austin Long, "Red Glare: The Origin and Implications of Russia's New Nuclear Weapons," *War on the Rocks*, March 26, 2018b. As of June 18, 2018:
https://warontherocks.com/2018/03/red-glare-the-origin-and-implications-of-russias-new-nuclear-weapons

[22] For more detailed discussion, see Brendan Rittenhouse Green and Austin Long, "The MAD Who Wasn't There: Soviet Reactions to the Late Cold War Nuclear Balance," *Security Studies*, Vol. 26, No. 4, 2017. See also the declassified report by the President's Foreign Intelligence Advisory Board, "The Soviet 'War Scare,'" February 15, 1990. As of June 18, 2018: https://nsarchive2.gwu.edu/nukevault/ebb533-The-Able-Archer-War-Scare-Declassified-PFIAB-Report-Released/

[23] See Long, 2018b.

campaigns.[24] Moreover, the Russians believe the United States would be more likely to use conventional weapons in a first strike, making such a strike more likely than one that would have to rely on nuclear weapons.

The second difference is the emergence of so-called "color revolutions" on the Russian periphery—successful uprisings against Moscow-friendly regimes that the Russians believe the United States helped engineer.[25] Together, these two new fears have led Russian leadership to fear U.S.-sponsored unrest (as Russian leaders believe happened in Ukraine), backed up with precision munitions supplied by the United States and its allies. The Russians think they have seen this movie before in Serbia, Libya, Iraq, and, if not for timely Russian intervention, Syria.

This combination of new and old fears about the United States, whether justified or not, has shaped Russian nuclear strategy and forces. Crucially, these fears also could help precipitate a nuclear crisis between the United States and Russia, even if neither side truly has aggressive intentions. Russian leaders could perceive unrest or revolution in one of its neighbors (e.g., Belarus) as engineered by the United States and take what it believes to be appropriate defensive measures. U.S. and NATO leaders could take what from their perspective are equally defensive measures, resulting in a crisis and possible conflict.

Moreover, if conflict did happen, Russia might rapidly expend most of its non-nuclear military options. Its long-range precision strike arsenal, while capable, is not very large. Its offensive cyber and counterspace capabilities might likewise fail to terminate conflict and, as NATO mobilized, a conventional battle would inevitably begin to shift against Russia. Therefore, Russian military commanders might recommend limited nuclear use relatively quickly if non-nuclear capabilities failed to terminate the conflict promptly. Whether Russian political leaders would accept such a recommendation is unknowable, but this scenario underscores that, even if Russian intentions are largely defensive, nuclear crisis and even limited nuclear use is possible.[26] This possibility highlights the important but tenuous role of arms control, discussed in the final section.

Prospects for Arms Control

Given the foregoing, prospects for arms control are grim. The United States maintains Russia is in violation of the INF Treaty, and Russia has leveled counteraccusations, including that U.S. European Phased Adaptive Approach missile defense launchers could be used to launch Tomahawk cruise missiles. There has been essentially no progress on this deadlock since 2014.

---

[24] Thomas McCabe, "The Russian Perception of the NATO Aerospace Threat," *Air and Space Power Journal*, Vol. 30, No. 3, 2016.

[25] Nicholas Bouchet, "Russia's "Militarization" of Colour Revolutions," Center for Security Studies-ETH Zurich, January 2016.

[26] See also Scott Boston and Dara Massicot, *The Russian Way of Warfare: A Primer*, Santa Monica, Calif.: RAND Corporation, PE-231-A, 2017. As of June 18, 2018: https://www.rand.org/pubs/perspectives/PE231.html; and Christopher S. Chivvis, Andrew Radin, Dara Massicot, and Clinton Bruce Reach, *Strengthening Strategic Stability with Russia*, Santa Monica, Calif.: RAND Corporation, PE-234-OSD, 2017. As of June 18, 2018: https://www.rand.org/pubs/perspectives/PE234.html

In contrast, both sides agree they are broadly in compliance with New START limits of 700 deployed strategic launchers and 1,550 strategic warheads. Russia claims that in February 2018 (the deadline for meeting the treaty limits) it had deployed 1,444 warheads on 527 launchers.[27] The United States was likewise in compliance, though Russia has questioned some of the conversions intended to limit launcher numbers.

New START expires in 2021, although there is an option to extend it for five years with both parties' agreement. While there has been some discussion of New START extension, the progress of the dialogue appears frozen at present. The two sides have had sporadic contact on arms control issues, with strategic stability talks in Helsinki in September 2017. More recently, strategic stability was one of the topics of a meeting between Chairman of the Joint Chiefs of Staff General Joseph Dunford and Chief of the General Staff General Valery Gerasimov in June 2018.

Yet a fundamental impasse remains. From the U.S. perspective, as embodied in the 2018 NPR, Russia is an unrepentant violator of existing arms control agreements, most notably the INF Treaty. It may seek to use nuclear weapons for coercive purposes against the United States and its allies.[28] From the Russian perspective, the United States is a serial invader bent on destroying the Russian state (or at the very least Russian leadership). It is also seeking to neutralize Russia's strategic deterrent.

It is especially important to note that given Russia's long-standing fears, there is probably no future for formal, treaty-based U.S.-Russian arms control if the negotiations do not cover missile defense (with the possible exception of New START extension). The Russians sought unsuccessfully to include missile defense in New START negotiations. Today, with their "new" systems, they may believe they have a stronger bargaining position. Yet the United States would certainly want any new agreements to ensure Russia returns to compliance with the INF Treaty and to involve the two new Russian systems Putin revealed in March.

Given these divergent views, the instinct may be to simply walk away from arms control, allowing New START to expire and even withdrawing from the INF Treaty. While this is understandable, arms control can provide transparency and communication mechanisms that can help prevent nuclear crisis scenarios like the one described previously. For example, even as U.S.-Russia relations have grown tense, both sides have been able to undertake more than 130 onsite inspections while exchanging data thousands of times.[29]

The most comprehensive solution may be to start from scratch, with a broader set of negotiations that seeks new mutually acceptable limits on intermediate-range systems (to replace the INF Treaty), "new" Russian systems, and missile defenses. Yet the United States understandably seeks missile defenses against North Korea and Iran, even if it does not seek to neutralize Russia's strategic deterrent, as the Kremlin fears. Moreover, a comprehensive solution by its nature would likely take a very long time to negotiate.

---

[27] U.S. State Department, "New START Treaty Aggregate Numbers of Strategic Offensive Arms, fact sheet, February 22, 2018. As of June 18, 2018: https://www.state.gov/t/avc/newstart/278775.htm

[28] See U.S. Department of Defense, 2018, pp. xvii and 8.

[29] U.S. Department of State, "New Start Treaty Inspection Activities," webpage, undated. As of June 18, 2018: https://www.state.gov/t/avc/newstart/c52405.htm

Absent such a comprehensive solution, the current arms control regime between the United States and Russia will likely continue to fray. It seems very unlikely the Russian government, which does not acknowledge violating the INF Treaty, will change its behavior. The United States will thus be faced with a stark choice by 2021—maintain New START, which the Russians seem to be complying with, for as long as possible, despite Russian violation of the INF Treaty? Or allow New START to expire and possibly withdraw from the INF Treaty as well?

Maintaining New START will maintain valuable transparency and channels of communication, yet will *de facto* confirm to the Russians that the United States will treat each arms control issue separately. This could encourage further violations of INF and other treaties, as the Russians would believe New START would continue and that a successor treaty might even be possible in 2026. Russian leaders might even conclude the United States is so desperate for arms control that they could even violate New START in the future.

Allowing New START to expire would help disabuse Russian leaders of the idea of U.S. desperation and demonstrate that arms control violations have real consequences. Yet it would mean that for the first time in more than three decades that U.S.-Russian nuclear competition would be unrestrained. Neither side would have the clarity on the status of the other side's strategic forces that years of inspections and data exchanges have enabled.

Perhaps the key indicator will be how the Russians seek to present the two novel systems Putin revealed in March. New START includes a provision on novel systems:

> When a Party believes that a new kind of strategic offensive arm is emerging, that Party shall have the right to raise the question of such a strategic offensive arm for consideration in the Bilateral Consultative Commission.[30]

If the Russians are willing to address these two systems at the Bilateral Consultative Commission (or other official venue) for potential inclusion in New START limitations, then extension may make sense despite Russian violation of INF and other treaties. If the Russians are unwilling to engage in productive dialogue on these novel systems, it is hard to see a future for New START or indeed arms control generally.

---

[30] See Article V of the New Strategic Arms Reduction Treaty, Prague, 2010. As of June 18, 2018: https://www.state.gov/documents/organization/140035.pdf

Mr. POE. Thank you Dr. Long.
Dr. Kim?

STATEMENT OF PATRICIA M. KIM, PH.D., STANTON NUCLEAR SECURITY FELLOW, COUNCIL ON FOREIGN RELATIONS

Ms. KIM. Chairman Poe, Ranking Member Keating, members of the subcommittee thank you for the opportunity to testify today on China's nuclear posture, a complex and evolving topic that will have significant implications for the security of the United States, our allies, as well as global nonproliferation efforts.

First, with China's nuclear doctrine, China has historically sustained a relatively small nuclear arsenal that is focused on deterring a nuclear attack by maintaining a credible second strike capability, which means the ability to deliver a retaliatory nuclear strike in the response to an adversary's initial first attack. According to China's latest defense white paper published in 2015, the Chinese Government is committed to pursuing a defensive nuclear strategy and states that it intends to keep its nuclear capabilities at a minimum level that is solely focused on deterrence and stopping others from threatening China with nuclear weapons.

Since China conducted its first nuclear test in 1964, it has adopted a no-first-use policy, which commits to refrain from attacking any entity first with nuclear weapons and to never use or threaten the use of nuclear weapons against a non-nuclear weapons state. Some, however, have raised the question of whether China is truly committed to this no-first-use policy. They point to various debates within China with some Chinese strategists calling on Beijing to qualify this policy and exempt certain types of non-nuclear attacks or others saying that China should get rid of this policy altogether so that it could prevent others from challenging China's territorial claims.

But it is important to note that these arguments have been countered by other Chinese strategists who say that China's no-first-use policy has actually served its purpose well and that letting go of this policy would actually open up a can of worms. Also, it is important to note that these debates do not represent the official views of the Chinese Government, and they are usually carried on by retired military officials or academics within China.

But they do provide a window into the way China's nuclear strategy could evolve if more hawkish voices were to prevail in the future. While China doesn't release official information on its nuclear arsenal, it is believed to possess a small but expanding arsenal of about 280 nuclear warheads. In addition to adding about 40 nuclear warheads since 2010, Beijing has focused its efforts on advancing its nuclear delivery systems as part of its broader drive to become a world-class military power by 2049. These developments have included a MIRV-capable ICBMs as well as a ballistic missile submarine.

It is important, however, not to overstate China's nuclear capabilities and to place its nuclear modernization in the broader, comparative context. The United States and Russia still possess 90 percent of the world's nuclear weapons and are in the midst of their own nuclear modernization programs. Furthermore, China lags far behind the United States in terms of its nuclear delivery capabilities.

Barring fundamental changes in China's internal or external environment that wholly transform China's nuclear calculus, it is unlikely that China will shift away from its emphasis on minimum deterrents and strive to reach parity with the United States' nuclear capabilities in the foreseeable future. It is also vital to note that the United States actually has the greatest influence on the trajectory of China's nuclear force modernization. Beijing is especially wary of U.S. capabilities that can challenge its minimum deterrent and is watching closely what we do with ballistic missile defense and theater missile defense. And Beijing firmly believes that theater missile defense especially is a U.S. tool that is meant to contain China.

On arms control, I will save my remarks since I am running out of time for the Q&A, but China is a part of several or most multilateral arms control agreements. And in terms of nonproliferation, China in the past has contributed to proliferation, but it has become more conservative in recent years especially as it consolidates its great power status. And since joining the NPT in 1992, China states that it opposes nuclear proliferation. Obviously, it has not lived up to these commitments, and the U.S. has fined or sanctioned Chinese entities, for instance, for engaging in proliferating activities so there are certainly concerns there.

Let me move to my policy recommendations briefly. I would like to remark that as China begins to modernize its nuclear weapons arsenals, I think it is very important for us to engage in bilateral confidence building and avoid spurring an action/reaction dynamic. At the same time, it is very important to strengthen our alliances and reassure our allies as they watch China grow its arsenal and also its conventional capabilities. And also it is very important to leverage China's desire for stability.

So China, Xi Jinping, has set out many ambitious goals for his country, and none of these can be met if a nuclear war was to break out on China's borders because of a crisis on the Korean Peninsula, for instance. So I think it is very important for the U.S. leaders to push Chinese leaders to do more in terms of nonproliferation for their own strategic interests.

And finally, I think it is very important for the United States to set a leading tone on arms control. As a responsible great power, the United States should lead the charge and not introduce new nuclear weapons, work to raise the threshold for nuclear conflict, and continue to rally its counterparts to work toward reducing and ultimately ridding the world of nuclear weapons. Thank you very much.

[The prepared statement of Ms. Kim follows:]

COUNCIL *on*
FOREIGN
RELATIONS

June 21, 2018

Chinese Perceptions on Nuclear Weapons, Arms Control and Nonproliferation

Prepared statement by
Patricia M. Kim
Stanton Nuclear Security Fellow
Council on Foreign Relations

Before the
Subcommittee on Terrorism, Nonproliferation, and Trade, United States House
Foreign Affairs Committee
United States House of Representatives
2nd Session, *115th* Congress

Hearing on "Russian and Chinese Nuclear Arsenals: Posture, Proliferation, and the Future of Arms Control"

Chairman Poe, Ranking Member Keating, distinguished members of the committee, thank you for the opportunity to testify on China's nuclear posture, a complex and evolving topic that has significant implications for the security of the United States, its allies, and global nonproliferation efforts. My testimony will address China's nuclear doctrine and the current state of its nuclear arsenal, its views on arms control, and its record on nonproliferation. I will conclude with several policy recommendations based on my analysis of these issues.

CHINA'S NUCLEAR DOCTRINE AND NUCLEAR ARSENAL

China's Nuclear Doctrine

China has historically sustained a relatively small nuclear arsenal that is focused on deterring a nuclear attack by maintaining a reliable second-strike capability—i.e. the ability to deliver a retaliatory nuclear strike in response to an adversary's initial nuclear attack. Such a strategy requires robust surveillance and radar capabilities to facilitate early detection, the survivability of nuclear forces from an incoming attack, and counter-strike capabilities that can penetrate an adversary's missile defense system and inflict significant damage.[1] According to China's latest defense white paper published in 2015, the Chinese government is

---

[1] Nan Li, "China's Evolving Nuclear Strategy: Will China Drop 'No First Use?'" *China Brief* 18, no. 1 (2018). https://jamestown.org/program/chinas-evolving-nuclear-strategy-will-china-drop-no-first-use/.

committed to pursuing a defensive nuclear strategy and intends to keep its nuclear capabilities at a "minimum level" that is solely focused on deterring others from threatening China with nuclear weapons.[2]

Since China conducted its first nuclear test in 1964, it has adopted a 'no first use' policy which commits it to refrain from attacking any entity first with nuclear weapons, and to never use or threaten the use of nuclear weapons against a non-nuclear-weapons state. China's latest defense white paper released in 2015 reaffirms this policy.[3]

Some have raised the question of whether China will remain committed to its 'no first use' policy, pointing to debates among Chinese strategists on the utility of upholding such a policy. For instance, some Chinese strategists have called on Beijing to qualify its 'no first use' policy by exempting certain types of non-nuclear attacks that cause extreme destruction or situations in which China's conventional forces are unable to defend against a large-scale foreign invasion. Others have called for abandoning the policy all together to deter states from challenging China's territorial claims. These arguments have been countered by Chinese strategists who contend abandoning the 'no first use' policy would actually increase China's vulnerability and damage its international image, among other consequences. It is important to note that these debates are largely fueled by retired military officials and academics within China and do not represent official views of the Chinese government. However, they do provide a window into how China's nuclear strategy could evolve if more hawkish voices were to prevail.[4]

Present State of China's Nuclear Arsenal and Delivery Systems

While China does not release official information on its nuclear arsenal, it is believed to possess a small but expanding arsenal of about 280 nuclear warheads.[5] In addition to adding about 40 warheads to its arsenal since 2010, Beijing has also focused its efforts on advancing its nuclear delivery systems in recent years as part of its broader drive to expand its military capabilities to become a "fully-developed great power" by 2049.[6]

China's nuclear modernization program has focused primarily on increasing the survivability of its nuclear forces and increasing retaliatory capability. Most notably, China has shifted away from its older liquid-fueled, silo-based missiles to road-mobile, solid-fueled missiles, and has developed multiple independently targetable re-entry vehicle (MIRV) capable intercontinental ballistic missiles (ICBM) that boost its ability to penetrate missile defense systems. China has also developed a ballistic missile submarine (SSBN) in recent years, giving Beijing access to a new sea-based nuclear deterrent.[7] In the coming years, China will continue to "optimize its

---

[2] *China's Military Strategy*, State Council of the People's Republic of China, May 27, 2015
http://english.gov.cn/archive/white_paper/2015/05/27/content_281475115610833.htm.
[3] Ibid.
[4] Eric Heginbotham et al., *China's Evolving Nuclear Deterrent: Major Drivers and Issues for the United States* (Santa Monica: Rand Corporation, 2017), 129-33,
https://www.rand.org/content/dam/rand/pubs/research_reports/RR1600/RR1628/RAND_RR1628.pdf. See also Li, "China's Evolving Nuclear Strategy," and see *Annual Report to Congress:*
Military and Security Developments Involving the People's Republic of China 2017, U.S. Department of Defense, 2017, 60,
https://www.defense.gov/Portals/1/Documents/pubs/2017_China_Military_Power_Report.PDF.
[5] This estimate comes from the Stockholm International Peace Research Institute's *SIPRI Yearbook 2018* (Oxford University Press, 2018), https://sipri.org/media/press-release/2018/modernization-nuclear-weapons-continues-number-peacekeepers-declines-new-sipri-yearbook-out-now.
[6] For an overview of China's general military expansion, see *Understanding China's Military Expansion and Implications for U.S. Policy. Hearing on China's Worldwide Military Expansion, Before the House Permanent Select Committee on Intelligence*, 115th Cong. (2018) (Statement of Patricia M. Kim), https://cfrds-files.cfr.org/sites/default/files/report_pdf/Patricia%20Kim%20-%20Testimony%20on%20China%20Military%20Expansion%20-%20HPSCI%20May%2017.pdf.
[7] Hans M. Kristensen and Robert S. Norris, "Chinese nuclear forces," *Bulletin of the Atomic Scientists* 72, no. 4 (2016), 205-211,
https://www.tandfonline.com/doi/pdf/10.1080/00963402.2016.1194054

nuclear force structure, improve strategic early warning, command and control, missile penetration, rapid reaction, and survivability and protection," as declared in its 2015 defense white paper. [8]

It is important, however, not to overstate China's nuclear capabilities and to place its nuclear modernization in the broader comparative context. The United States and Russia still possess an overwhelming majority—over 90 percent—of the world's nuclear weapons and are in the midst of their own nuclear modernization programs.[9] Furthermore, China lags far behind the United States in terms of nuclear delivery capabilities. For instance, the PLA Air Force still does not have a nuclear mission although a strategic bomber with a nuclear delivery capability is currently under development. As a result, China is limited to a land and sea-based nuclear force structure, unlike the United States which also has strategic aircraft capabilities.[10] Barring fundamental changes in China's internal or external environment that wholly transform China's nuclear calculus, it is unlikely China will abandon its emphasis on minimum deterrence and strive to reach parity with the United States' nuclear capabilities in the foreseeable future.[11]

It is also vital to note that the United States has the greatest influence on the trajectory of China's nuclear force modernization.[12] Beijing is especially wary of U.S. capabilities that can challenge its minimum nuclear deterrent and its retaliatory-strike capabilities. As such, the United States' expansion of ballistic missile defense and prompt global strike capabilities in particular have raised concerns about vulnerability in Beijing.[13] Chinese strategists insist that these developments hinder smaller nuclear powers (like China) from pursuing nuclear disarmament and instead force them to enhance their own retaliatory-strike capabilities. Beijing is especially wary of the expansion of the United States' theater missile defense systems in East Asia, which is sees as a means to contain China. The United States efforts to develop a conventional prompt global strike capability has also raised concerns about preserving China's retaliation capabilities. As the United States continues to develop ballistic missile defense and global strike capabilities, Chinese enhancements of its own nuclear weapons system will follow.[14]

CHINA'S VIEWS ON ARMS CONTROL AND NONPROLIFERATION

China's Participation in Multilateral Arms Control Agreements

China is party to several major multilateral arms control agreements and treaties, including the Nuclear Nonproliferation Treaty, the Convention on Physical Protection of Nuclear Material, the Chemical Weapons Convention, the Biological Weapons Convention, and the International Convention for the Suppression of Acts of Nuclear Terrorism. China has signed but not ratified the Comprehensive Test Ban Treaty. China is also a member of the Nuclear Suppliers Group, the International Atomic Energy Agency, and the Global Initiative to Combat Nuclear Terrorism. Despite the rejection of its membership to the Missile Technology Control Regime in 2004 on the grounds that China does not adequately restrict missile and technology exports, China has pledged to abide by the rules of the group.

China is not a participant in the Hague Code of Conduct against Ballistic Missile Proliferation or the Proliferation Security Initiative (PSI). Beijing has chosen not to participate in PSI, which aims to stop

---

[8] *China's Military Strategy*, 2015.
[9] *SIPRI Yearbook 2018.*
[10] *Annual Report to Congress: Military and Security Developments Involving the People's Republic of China 2017*, 61.
[11] See Gregory Kulacki, *The Chinese Military Updates China's Nuclear Strategy* (Cambridge: Union of Concerned Scientists, 2015), https://www.ucsusa.org/sites/default/files/attach/2015/03/chinese-nuclear-strategy-full-report.pdf and "David Logan, Hard Constraints on China's Nuclear Forces," *War on the Rocks*, November 8, 2017, https://warontherocks.com/2017/11/china-nuclear-weapons-breakout/. See also Heginbotham et al., *China's Evolving Nuclear Deterrent*, 38, 47, 129-133.
[12] Heginbotham et al., 57.
[13] Kulacki, 5.
[14] Heginbotham et al., 61-68.

trafficking of weapons of mass destruction (WMD) by increasing interdiction efforts on the grounds that interdictions may "go beyond the international law."[15] China's reluctance to participate has been rooted more directly in its desire not to alienate North Korea, a principle target of PSI, and in its principled objection against what it views as the selective targeting of certain regimes like North Korea and Iran, but not others, like India and Israel.[16]

Prospects for China's Participation in Arms Reductions Negotiations

Prospects for arms control dialogues with China remain dim given the reality that China has a dramatically smaller nuclear arsenal compared to the United States and Russia. First, negotiations require an open accounting of existing capabilities. China is reluctant to embrace full transparency, given its desire to maintain opacity to enhance the survivability of its small nuclear arsenal.[17] In addition, Chinese strategists insist that Washington and Moscow must first commit to significant reductions in their own arsenals before asking China to reduce its weapons.[18] Given strained U.S.-Russia relations and accusations on both sides of violations of the Intermediate-range Nuclear Forces Treaty, the appetite for new arms control initiatives between Washington and Moscow seems non-existent in the near-term, which means arms control dialogue with China will also be difficult to pursue.[19]

China and Nonproliferation

According to China's 2005 white paper on arms control, disarmament, and nonproliferation, China "firmly opposes the proliferation of weapons of mass destruction and their means of delivery" and has "actively participated" in international non-proliferation efforts by tightening export controls and law enforcement.[20] In practice, however, China has not always lived up to these commitments. The United States has long been concerned about China's involvement in the proliferation of WMD and its laxity in nonproliferation efforts. Chinese entities, such as state-owned defense industrial corporations, are known to have aided Pakistan's nuclear and missile programs throughout the 1990s, in addition to providing sensitive technologies and materials to Saudi Arabia, Iran, Libya, and North Korea.[21] China's willingness to assist the nuclear programs of other states in the past were driven by both strategic motives, such as the desire to arm Pakistan to balance against India, a mutual rival, as well as economic incentives that overrode concerns about proliferation and nuclear terrorism.[22]

Since the early 2000s, China has expressed greater willingness to crack down on proliferation through official statements and measures to tighten export controls. While Beijing participated in the maximum pressure campaign against North Korea to an unprecedented degree this past year, it has customarily been unwilling to

---

[15] "The Proliferation Security Initiative," Ministry of Foreign Affairs of the People's Republic of China, April 7, 2011, http://www.fmprc.gov.cn/mfa_eng/wjb_663304/zzjg_663340/jks_665232/kjlc_665236/fkswt_665240/t410725.shtml

[16] Bates Gill, "China and Nuclear Arms Control: Current Positions and Future Policies," *SIPRI Insights on Peace and Security* (April 2010), 6
https://www.sipri.org/sites/default/files/files/insight/SIPRIInsight1004.pdf

[17] Hui Zhang, "A Discussion of China's Nuclear Transparency Options." Paper, 42nd Annual Meeting of the Institute for Nuclear Materials Management (July 2001). 2 https://www.belfercenter.org/sites/default/files/files/publication/inmm01-chinatrans.pdf

[18] Heginbotham et al., 153.

[19] Steven Pifer, "The Death of the INF Treaty Could Signal a U.S.-Russia Missile Race," *The National Interest*, December 6, 2017, http://nationalinterest.org/feature/the-death-the-inf-treaty-could-signal-us-russia-missile-race-23532

[20] "China issues white paper on arms control, disarmament & non-proliferation," Mission of the People's Republic of China to the European Union, http://www.chinamission.be/eng/zywj/bps/t1255353.htm

[21] Shirley A. Kan , "China and Proliferation of Weapons of Mass Destruction and Missiles: Policy Issues," Congressional Research Service, January 5, 2015, https://fas.org/sgp/crs/nuke/RL31555.pdf. See also "The Missile Technology Control Regime at a Glance," Arms Control Association, July 2017, https://www.armscontrol.org/factsheets/inter

[22] Li Bin, "Chinese Thinking on Nuclear Weapons," Arms Control Association, December 2015, https://www.armscontrol.org/ACT/2015_12/Features/Chinese-Thinking-On-Nuclear-Weapons

sign onto expansive sanctions on its traditional security partners. For instance, Beijing has often shielded Pyongyang in the past from crippling sanctions, given its desire not to destabilize the Kim regime. These tendencies have also been reinforced by disgruntlement with the fact that the economic burden of pressuring North Korea falls largely on China's shoulders.

China's lax enforcement of existing sanctions has driven the U.S. government to impose sanctions on Chinese companies over the years.[23] According to the State Department's compliance report on arms control, nonproliferation, and disarmament agreements and commitments released earlier this year, "Chinese entities continued to supply missile programs of proliferation concern" in 2017.[24] While it is unlikely that these entities were directed by the central government to engage in transactions that violate sanctions, the Chinese government has not always done its utmost to constrain various domestic entities who are most likely motivated by economic profit. And laxity is consistent with Beijing's desire to prioritize stability above all. Instead of using punitive measures, Beijing often pushes for "equal-footed dialogue" to "remove the root causes of nuclear terrorism and nuclear proliferation."[25] However, Beijing will cooperate on sanctions and enforcement if and when it deems doing so will prevent greater instability, as it judged during the tense months of late last year and early this year when North Korea's successive nuclear and missile tests and the Trump administration's threats to launch a limited military strike against Pyongyang spurred unparalleled Chinese cooperation in the maximum pressure campaign.

While China may not be a model state when it comes to efforts for nonproliferation, it will most likely start to adopt a more responsible attitude as it consolidates its great power status and its global interests grow. As China's economic and military footprint abroad increases, its citizens and assets will become more vulnerable nuclear terrorism and proliferation-related threats. As such we can expect China to take a more conservative approach on nuclear proliferation in the coming years.

POLICY RECOMMENDATIONS

Based on these observations of China's nuclear doctrine and arsenal, and its views on arms control and nonproliferation, I would like to suggest the following policy recommendations:

> **Engage in bilateral confidence building and avoid spurring an action-reaction dynamic.** As discussed above, China's nuclear force modernization will largely be influenced by the United States' own efforts to modernize its nuclear trajectory. As such, the United States should seek to engage in high-level dialogues with China to clarify respective nuclear policies, doctrine and capabilities, and to engage in confidence building measures to reduce the prospects of an action-reaction arms race that will not only be destabilizing for the world, but also prove highly costly for U.S. taxpayers. On a related note, the United States should think holistically about developing ballistic missile defense and pursuing new nuclear and non-nuclear capabilities that can increase the strategic vulnerability of other states.

> **Strengthen alliances and the credibility of the United States' security commitments.** China will continue to modernize its nuclear forces into the foreseeable future in order to maintain its minimum deterrent capabilities in the nuclear realm, and as part of its larger campaign to strengthen its military capabilities. In the midst of China's military expansion, it is vital the United States reassures its allies, especially in East Asia, of the credibility of its security commitments by clarifying and reinforcing its

---

[23] "Iran, North Korea, and Syria Nonproliferation Act: Imposed Sanctions," U.S. Department of State, May 29, 2013, https://www.state.gov/t/isn/inksna/c28836.htm
[24] "2018 Report on Adherence to and Compliance With Arms Control, Nonproliferation, and Disarmament Agreements and Commitments," U.S. Department of State, https://www.state.gov/t/avc/rls/rpt/2018/280532.htm
[25] "Statement by H.E. Xi Jinping President of the People's Republic of China at the Nuclear Security Summit," Ministry of Foreign Affairs of the People's Republic of China, http://www.fmprc.gov.cn/mfa_eng/wjdt_665385/zyjh_665391/t1140583.shtml

security assurances, conducting joint exercises to strengthen alliance capabilities and interoperability, and resolving disputes with allies in a discreet and cooperative manner. Neglecting our allies could drive these states to develop their own nuclear weapons on the one hand, triggering a dangerous arms race in the East Asian region, or force them to accommodate China's demands on the other hand, at the expense of alliance solidarity. The United States' alliances are an invaluable asset that enable Washington to lead collective challenges against Chinese aggression and to generally shape outcomes in the global arena, and their maintenance must be prioritized.

➢ **Leverage China's desire for stability and its growing international profile and interests to encourage its active participation in nonproliferation efforts.** Chinese President Xi Jinping has set out ambitious goals to develop China into a world class power by 2049. None of these goals can be achieved if China is beset with chaos and instability, such as a war stemming from a nuclear crisis on the Korean Peninsula. Furthermore, as more and more Chinese assets and citizens move abroad, they will also become increasingly vulnerable to nuclear terrorism and other proliferation-related instability. U.S. leaders should leverage China's desire for stability and its need to protect its growing interests to encourage Beijing to do more to curb nuclear proliferation.

➢ **Set a leading tone on arms control.** The United States' most recent Nuclear Posture Review announced that it would introduce two new types of nuclear weapons in light of the growing threat from China and Russia, among other actors. As a responsible great power, the United States should instead lead the charge against introducing new nuclear weapons, work to raise the threshold for nuclear conflict, and continue to rally its counterparts to work toward reducing and ultimately ridding the world of nuclear weapons.

ESTIMATE OF GLOBAL NUCLEAR WEAPONS
IN JANUARY 2018

Source. SIPRI Yearbook 2018

Mr. POE. Thank you Dr. Kim.

Mr. Rose?

STATEMENT OF THE HONORABLE FRANK ROSE, SENIOR FELLOW, SECURITY AND STRATEGY, FOREIGN POLICY PROGRAM, THE BROOKINGS INSTITUTION (FORMER ASSISTANT SECRETARY FOR ARMS CONTROL, VERIFICATION, AND COMPLIANCE, U.S. DEPARTMENT OF STATE)

Mr. ROSE. Chairman Poe, Ranking Member Keating, members of the subcommittee, it is an honor to appear before you today to discuss Russian and Chinese strategic capabilities and their implications for U.S. strategy and arms control. Let me begin by stating that although I am currently a senior fellow at The Brookings Institution, I am testifying today in my personal capacity.

As my colleague, Thomas Wright, notes in his recent book, All Measures Short of War, the United States is in competition with Russia and China for the future of the international order. As part of that competition, Russia and China are modernizing their nuclear forces and are also developing new disruptive technologies. In my testimony today I want to hit three areas. First, Russian and Chinese nuclear modernization programs; second, Russia and China's development of asymmetric capabilities such as offensive cyber and counter space; and then, finally, provide you a few recommendations on how the United States should respond.

Now Dr. Long and Dr. Kim, I think, did a nice job at outlining the Russian and Chinese nuclear threat, and I am in general agreement with that. I go into more detail in my written statement. So I really want to focus on the latter two points: Offensive cyber and counter space as well as my recommendations for the United States.

Russia and China understand that the United States is dependent on cyber and outer space capabilities. Therefore, they are developing a series of offensive cyber and counter space capabilities designed to degrade-defeat-destroy U.S. space in cyber space networks. These types of asymmetric capabilities could have significant implications for strategic deterrents, especially nuclear command, control, and communications.

The United States requires a comprehensive strategy to effectively manage the strategic challenge from Russia and China. The foundation of that strategy must be to maintain a safe, secure, and effective strategic nuclear deterrent. Therefore, I recommend the United States take the following steps as part of that strategy: Complete the modernization of its strategic nuclear delivery systems and supporting infrastructure, enhance the resiliency of our outer space, cyber, and undersea communications infrastructure, and maintain the cohesions of our alliances.

From a geopolitical perspective, the U.S. system of alliances is one of our asymmetric advantages and something that neither Russia or China possess. And from a military perspective, the United States needs our allies to defend the U.S. homeland from strategic threats. Indeed, radars, communication stations, and relay ground stations based on allied territory are critical to the strategic deterrents and homeland missile defense missions. Furthermore, we should extend the New START Treaty and explore the role that arms control may play in helping manage great power competition in the future.

We also need to engage Russia and China in bilateral dialogues focused on reducing the risk of nuclear miscalculation and promoting stability. We need to advance a broader international conversation about strategic stability that includes other strategic actors such as Britain, France, India, and Pakistan. We need to develop norms of responsible behavior to help manage competition in a merging domain such as outer space and cyber. And, finally, we need to explore whether the United States Government, in particular the Departments of State and Defense, is structured in a way to appropriately allow the United States to effectively manage great power competition in the strategic domain.

Thank you very much, Mr. Chairman, and I look forward to your questions.

[The prepared statement of Mr. Rose follows:]

Statement of the Honorable Frank A. Rose
Senior Fellow for Security and Strategy
The Brookings Institution

House Subcommittee on Terrorism, Nonproliferation, and Trade
"Russian and Chinese Nuclear Arsenals: Posture, Proliferation, and the Future of Arms Control"
June 21, 2018

Introduction

Chairman Poe, Ranking Member Keating, and members of the subcommittee, it is an honor to appear before you today to discuss Russian and Chinese strategic capabilities, and their implications for U.S. strategy and arms control. Let me begin by stating that although I am currently a senior fellow for security and strategy at the Brookings Institution, I am presenting testimony representing my personal views. As an independent think tank, the Brookings Institution does not take institutional positions on any issue.

The 2018 Nuclear Posture Review (NPR) states "that global threat conditions have worsened markedly since the 2010 NPR…The United States faces a more diverse and advanced nuclear-threat environment than ever before."[1] In particular, the NPR highlights the return of great power competition. As my colleague, Thomas Wright, notes in his recent book, *All Measures Short of War: The Contest for 21st Century and the Future of American Power*, "The United States is in competition with Russia and China for the future of the international order."[2] Russia and China are also modernizing their nuclear forces and developing new and disruptive counterspace and offensive cyber capabilities.

Indeed, strategic stability in the emerging security environment no longer follows the two-state (e.g., United States and the Soviet Union), one-weapon (e.g., nuclear weapons) model of the Cold War. Today's security environment includes multiple states and additional capabilities such as counterspace and offensive cyber weapons. How does the United States manage this competition in a way that allows the United States to effectively deter potential adversaries, maintain strategic stability, and reduce the risk of nuclear use?

To effectively respond to the Russian and Chinese challenge and the emergence of disruptive technologies, the United States will need to *complete* the modernization of its strategic nuclear forces; *enhance* the resiliency of its space and cyber infrastructure; *maintain* the cohesion and effectiveness of its alliances; *engage* Russia and China in bilateral strategic stability dialogues; *pursue* pragmatic arms control initiatives focused enhancing stability and predictability; *begin* a broader international dialogue on strategic stability that includes

---

[1] U.S. Department of Defense, "Nuclear Posture Review 2018," (Arlington. VA: U.S. Department of Defense, February 2018), p. 9, https://media.defense.gov/2018/Feb/02/2001872886/-1/-1/1/2018-NUCLEAR-POSTURE-REVIEW-FINAL-REPORT.PDF.

[2] Thomas Wright, *All Measures Short of War: The Contest for the 21st Century and the Future of American Power*, (New Haven, CT: Yale University Press, 2017), 189.

additional actors (i.e., the members of the P-5, India, Pakistan); and ***develop*** norms of responsible behavior for emerging domains such as outer space and cyber.

The Russian Federation

Russia's view of the strategic environment and role of nuclear weapons

Any review of Russian nuclear policy needs to begin with an understanding of its overall geopolitical situation. Despite its aggressive actions in Ukraine and Syria, Russia faces significant long-term security challenges.

First, Russia possesses no allies or durable security partners. Yes, Russia does have Lukashenko in Belarus and Assad in Syria, but I would not describe either of those countries or leaders as particularly reliable partners. On the other hand, the United States has numerous alliances and strategic partnerships with countries around the world. Second, Russia continues to face serious demographic challenges and as a result, Russia no longer possesses the strategic weight of numbers it once had.[3]

Third, Russia lacks a modern and innovative civilian economy. Besides oil and gas, what does Russia export on the civilian market? I can't recall many items. Indeed, Russia has always had a challenge transferring its strong scientific research base into innovative commercial products.

Fourth, while there's no doubt that Russian conventional capabilities have improved since the early 2000's, which we've seen demonstrated most recently in Syria, I don't think any serious military analyst would argue that Russia's military capabilities are on par with that of the United States at the global level.

And finally, Russia remains concerned about growing Chinese political, economic, and military power in Eurasia. Though Russia and China currently have a "strategic partnership," that partnership is fundamentally about one thing: balancing the global power and influence of the United States. Any student of Sino-Russian relations knows that this is a very complicated relationship with numerous peaks and valleys throughout its history. If you scrape beneath the surface, it becomes evident that there are longer-term tensions between Russia and China.

Given these host of strategic challenges, we must ask ourselves the question: how will Russia guarantee its security over the long-term? In my view, the answer is very clear: nuclear weapons.

Since the end of the Cold War in 1991, Democratic and Republican administrations have sought to reduce of role of nuclear weapons in U.S. defense strategy. However, the Russian national security establishment has not shared this view. Indeed, as the U.S. National Intelligence Council noted in 2012:

---

[3] http://worldpopulationreview.com/countries/russia-population/

Nuclear ambitions in the U.S. and Russia over the last 20 years have evolved in opposite directions. Reducing the role of nuclear weapons in U.S. security strategy is a U.S. objective, while Russia is pursuing new concepts and capabilities for expanding the role of nuclear weapons in its security strategy.[4]

The Soviet Union's primary motivation for pursuing nuclear reductions was driven by the need to reduce tensions with the United States so it could invest greater resources into the revitalization of its civilian economy. And Russia's subsequent pursuit of nuclear arms control agreements was driven by a desire to maintain strategic nuclear parity with the United States at a time of significant economic distress.

For example, Russia did not sign the New Strategic Arms Reduction Treaty (New START) because it believed in "a world free of nuclear weapons." It does not. Rather, New START was fundamentally about maintaining strategic nuclear parity with the United States, capping the number of deployed U.S. nuclear warheads, and providing Russia insights into the U.S. strategic nuclear arsenal that it would not have access to without the Treaty.

Additionally, Russia has expressed zero interest in pursuing further strategic nuclear reductions, or even beginning a discussion about non-strategic nuclear weapons, which are not limited by New START, and where Russia enjoys a large numerical advantage. This position is driven by several factors. First, Russia believes that emerging technologies such a missile defense, outer space, and the rise of increasingly accurate conventional strike systems are reshaping the strategic balance. Therefore, they argue that these types of military capabilities must be part of any future strategic arms control discussion. Russia is particularly concerned about the possible deployment of space-based missile defenses by the United States, which Russia views as an "existential threat" to the long-term viability of its strategic nuclear deterrent. Second, while the Obama administration had called for negotiating an additional round of bilateral strategic nuclear reductions, Russia opposed this, arguing that any future nuclear arms reduction process must be multilateral and include China, France, and the United Kingdom.

Russian strategic nuclear modernization programs

Russia has been modernizing its strategic nuclear forces for over a decade. The most important element of its modernization program has been the development of new land-based intercontinental missiles (ICBMs) armed multiple independent re-entry vehicles (MIRVs). Overall, sixty percent of Russia's strategic deterrent is deployed on land-based systems. The two primary ICBM modernization programs include the road-mobile Yars (SS-27 Mod 2) and the Sarmat (SS-30), which is reportedly carries up to 10 MIRVs.[5]

Russia is also modernizing the sea- and air-based elements of its deterrent. For example, it is building eight new Borei-class ballistic missile submarines (SSBNs), modernizing its aging fleet of strategic TU-160 and TU-95 bombers, and deploying a new nuclear-armed cruise missile, the KH-101.[6] In addition to aforementioned systems, the 2018 NPR notes that Russia is

---

[4] Nuclear Posture Review, Arlington, p. 9.
[5] Shannon Kile and Hans Kristensen, "Trends in World Nuclear Forces, 2017," SIPRI Fact Sheet, July 2017, p.3.
[6] Ibid, p.3-4.

also developing at least two new intercontinental range systems: a hypersonic glide vehicle; and a new intercontinental, nuclear-armed, nuclear-powered, undersea autonomous torpedo.[7] It appears that these new systems are designed to ensure that Russian nuclear forces can penetrate any future U.S. missile defense system.

That said, Russia's strategic modernization program appears to be consistent with its obligations under New START. Indeed, the U.S. Department of State's annual New START report states: "Based on information available on December 31, 2017, the United States certifies that the Russian Federation is in compliance with New START."[8]

Russian non-strategic nuclear modernization programs

Russia is also modernizing its non-strategic nuclear forces. According to the NPR, Russia "is building a large, diverse, and modern set of non-strategic systems that are dual-capable" and that "these theater- and tactical-range systems are not accountable under the New START Treaty."[9] The NPR also notes that "Moscow believes these systems may provide useful options for escalation advantage."[10]

Of particular concern is Russia's development of a new ground-launched cruise missile (GLCM), the SSC-8, which is a direct violation of its obligations under the 1987 Intermediate Nuclear Forces (INF) Treaty. In the July 2014 edition of the U.S. Department of State's annual Arms Control Compliance Report, the United States declared that the Russian Federation was in violation of its obligations under the INF Treaty not to possess, produce, or flight test a ground-launched cruise missile (GLCM) with a range capability of 500 km to 5,500 km, or to produce launchers of such missiles.[11] Despite diplomatic efforts by both the Obama and Trump administrations to bring Russia back into compliance with the treaty, to date, those efforts have been unsuccessful.

At a March 8, 2017 hearing of the House Armed Services Committee, General Paul Selva, vice chairman of the Joint Chiefs of Staff, confirmed that Russia has moved forward with the deployment of that system. Selva stated: "We believe that the Russians have deployed a land-based cruise missile that violates the spirit and intent of the Intermediate Nuclear Forces Treaty."[12]

I believe it is unlikely that Russia will return to compliance with the INF Treaty. As I testified before this subcommittee last year, Russia's violation of the INF Treaty must be addressed. In that testimony, I recommended that the United States and its allies take a number of specific actions in response to Russia's violation of the treaty that would hold critical Russian

---

[7] U.S. Department of Defense, "Nuclear Posture Review 2018," p.9.
[8] U.S. Department of State, Annual Report on Implementation of the New Start Treaty, January 2018. https://www.state.gov/t/avc/rls/rpt/2018/280538.htm.
[9] Ibid
[10] Ibid.
[11] U.S. Department of State, *2014 Report on Adherence to and Compliance With Arms Control, Nonproliferation, and Disarmament Agreements and Commitments*, p. 8, July 2014.
[12] John M. Donnelly, "Hill Wants Answers on Russia's Fielding of New Missiles," *CQ Roll Call*, March 8, 2017.

assets at risk; maintain Alliance unity; and place the blame for the demise of the INF Treaty squarely where it belongs – with Russia.[13]

Russia's irresponsible rhetoric on nuclear weapons

Over the past several years, Russia has been extremely irresponsible regarding its public rhetoric on nuclear weapons. There have been several occasions where Russian officials have threatened to use nuclear weapons against U.S. allies. For example, in March 2015, the Russian ambassador to Denmark asserted that if Denmark allow its Navy to participate in the NATO missile defense system, Danish warships would become targets for Russian nuclear missiles.[14] That statement, and others like it, are totally unacceptable and do little to foster stability or reduce the risk of nuclear use. But one thing is clear: Russia views nuclear weapons as a way to intimidate and bully its neighbors. The NPR makes clear that the United States will respond to any first-use of nuclear weapons, stating that Russia should "understand that nuclear first use, however limited, will fail to achieve its objects, fundamentally alter the nature of a conflict, and trigger incalculable and intolerable costs for Moscow."[15]

The People's Republic of China

Chinese nuclear policy and doctrine

China's nuclear forces represent a fundamentally different challenge to the United States. While there is no doubt that China's nuclear capabilities represent a potential threat to the United States and its allies, I'm much less concerned about the evolution of Chinese nuclear forces and doctrine than I am with Russia's behavior.

Since achieving a nuclear weapons capability in 1964, China has maintained a "no first use" policy with regard to its nuclear arsenal. Under the policy, China will not to be the first to use nuclear weapons at any time or under any circumstances. Available evidence suggests this remains China's policy. Additionally, whereas Russia has made numerous public threats to use nuclear weapons against other nations, including several U.S. allies, China has not.

The primary challenge from China is its attempt to tilt the balance of power in the Western Pacific in its favor through a major conventional force build-up and development of anti-access, area denial and "asymmetric" capabilities (e.g., counter-space, cyber). While it is imperative that the United States continue to deter China's nuclear forces, our primary concern should be focused on countering China's efforts to gain conventional superiority in the Western Pacific.

---

[13] Frank Rose, "Testimony on the Future of the INF Treaty", Joint subcommittee hearing by the Committee on Foreign Affairs' Subcommittee on Terrorism, Nonproliferation, and Trade and the Committee on Armed Services' Subcommittee on Strategic Forces. March 30, 2017, https://foreignaffairs.house.gov/hearing/joint-subcommittee-hearing-consequences-context-russias-violations-inf-treaty/

[14] Reuters Staff, "Russian threatened to aim nuclear missiles at Denmark ships if it joins NATO shield," Reuters, March 22, 2015, https://www.reuters.com/article/us-denmark-russia/russia-threatens-to-aim-nuclear-missiles-at-denmark-ships-if-it-joins-nato-shield-idUSKBN0MI0ML20150322.

[15] Nuclear Posture Review, p. 30.

Chinese strategic nuclear modernization programs

Though China has been actively modernizing its strategic nuclear forces over a decade, at this point, we have seen no any evidence to suggest that it seeks to move beyond a "minimum deterrent" force or pursue strategic nuclear parity with the United States. For example, it is estimated that China has about 270 total nuclear warheads, as compared to approximately 4,000 warheads in the active U.S. nuclear stockpile."[16] According to Director of National Intelligence Dan Coats, China's strategic nuclear modernization program is "intended to ensure the viability of China's strategic deterrent by providing a second-strike capability.[17]" Indeed, the overarching characteristic of the modernization program is to ensure that China's nuclear forces become more survivable, ultimately by making them less vulnerable to a first-strike by another nuclear power.

The Chinese strategic nuclear modernization program consists of several elements. First, it is adding more survivable road-mobile ICBMs (e.g., DF-31A and DF-41) to its arsenal to complement its silo-based systems.[18] China is also continuing to improve the sea-based leg of its strategic deterrent. The JL-2 submarine-launched ballistic missile, which is currently under development, will provide China "its first long-range, sea-based nuclear capability." China has also tested a hypersonic glide vehicle and expressed its intention to develop a next generation nuclear-capable bomber.[19]

Like Russia, China is also concerned about the development of U.S. missile defenses and the potential impact of those systems on its strategic nuclear deterrent. Missile defense is most likely the driver behind China's decision to deploy MIRVs on some of its ICBMs. According to a 2017 report by the Stockholm International Peace Research Institute, "China has prioritized the deployment of MIRVs in order to improve its warhead penetration capabilities in response to advances in U.S. and, to a lesser extent, Indian missile defenses."[20]

Russian and Chinese offensive cyber and counterspace capabilities

In addition to their nuclear modernization programs, Russia and China are also actively developing offensive cyber and counterspace capabilities. Russia and China's development of these types of "asymmetric capabilities" could have significant implications for strategic deterrence, especially nuclear command, control, and communications (NC3) systems.In his testimony before the Senate Select Committee on Intelligence on February 13, 2018, Director of National Intelligence Daniel Coats highlighted the U.S. Intelligence Community's increasing concerns of Russia and China's development in the offensive cyber and counterspace arenas.

---

[16] Shannon Kile and Hans Kristensen, "Trends in World Nuclear Forces, 2017," SIPRI Fact Sheet, July 2017, p. 2.
[17] Coats, "Worldwide Threat Assessment," p. 7
[18] Ibid.
[19] Ibid
[20] Shannon Kile and Hans Kristensen, p. 5.

On Russian offensive cyber capabilities, Coats noted that in the coming year, it is likely that "Russia will conduct bolder and more disruptive cyber operations during the next year, most likely using new capabilities against Ukraine… In the next year, Russian intelligence and security services will continue to probe US and allied critical infrastructures.[21]" He also indicated that the U.S. Intelligence Community expects similar actions from China. Coats asserted: "China will continue to use cyber espionage and bolster cyber-attack capabilities to support national security priorities… China since 2015 has been advancing its cyber-attack capabilities by integrating its military cyber-attack and espionage resources in the Strategic Support Force, which it established in 2015."[22]

Regarding Russian and Chinese counterspace capabilities, Coats stated: "Both Russia and China continue to pursue antisatellite (ASAT) weapons as a means to reduce U.S. and allied military effectiveness… Military reforms in both countries in the past few years indicate an increased focus on establishing operational forces designed to integrate attacks against space systems and services with military operations in other domains."[23]

The United States Response to Russia and China

Modernize U.S. strategic nuclear forces and their supporting infrastructure

The United States requires a comprehensive strategy to effectively manage the strategic challenge from Russia and China. However, the foundation of that strategy must be continuing to maintain a safe, secure, and effective strategic nuclear deterrent.

In his April 2009 speech in Prague, former President Barack Obama outlined his long-term vision for peace and security in a world without nuclear weapons. But in that same speech, he also noted that as long as nuclear weapons existed, the United States would maintain a safe, secure, and effective deterrent. Therefore, under the Obama administration, the United States began a major recapitalization of its strategic nuclear delivery systems, nuclear command, control, and communications (NC3) system, and the Department of Energy nuclear infrastructure.

The Obama strategic nuclear modernization program included: the Columbia-class ballistic missile submarine (SSBN), the Ground-Based Strategic Deterrent (GBSD), the B-21 strategic bomber, and the Long-Range Stand-Off (LRSO) nuclear cruise missile. Additionally, the Obama administration began the modernization of the U.S. non-strategic nuclear capabilities, including the procurement of the nuclear-capable F-35 fighter and the B-61-12 nuclear gravity bomb. I believe it is critical that the United States move forward with the modernization of these nuclear delivery capabilities, the NC3 backbone, and the supporting DOE infrastructure.

The Trump administration's NPR essentially ratifies the Obama administration's strategic nuclear modernization program. However, the NPR recommended that the United States also "pursue select supplements" to the Obama administration's strategic nuclear modernization

---

[21] Coats, "Worldwide Threat Assessment," p. 5.

[22] Ibid

[23] Ibid, p.13.

program to "enhance the flexibility and responsiveness of U.S. nuclear forces."[24] These supplements include developing a new low-yield warhead for the D-5 submarine-launched ballistic missile (SLBM) and a new sea-launched cruise missile (SLCM) deployed on attack submarines and surface ships.

From my perspective, as long as the United States moves forward with modernization of the previously approved lower-yield capabilities (i.e., B-61-12 gravity bomb, and the LRSO nuclear cruise missile), that should be sufficient to deter the threat from Russia's non-strategic nuclear forces and other potential adversaries. In particular, I want to emphasize the importance of the LRSO nuclear cruise missile and the important stand-off capability that it provides. This stand-off capability will become increasingly important as Russia and China continue to improve their air defense capabilities.[25]

Enhance the resiliency of U.S. space, cyber, and other critical infrastructure

The U.S. nuclear command and control system is heavily dependent on access to outer space and cyber systems. As previously noted, Russia and China are dramatically improving their counterspace and offensive cyber capabilities. Therefore, it is critical that the United States finds ways to enhance the resiliency of these systems as it proceeds with the modernization of its nuclear forces. Indeed, the NPR directs the Department of Defense to strengthen the protection U.S. space-based assets. It also directs the DOD to "protect NC3 components against current and future cyber threats and ensure the continuity of U.S.-produced information technology necessary for the NC3 system."[26] Like the strategic nuclear modernization efforts, it is critical that Congress appropriate the necessary funds to enhance the United States' national security space and cyber infrastructure.

In addition to enhancing the resiliency of space and cyber capabilities, the United States also needs to pay close attention to the resiliency of the undersea cable communications network. Approximately 97% of the world's trans-oceanic communication transited over privately held, commercial, undersea fiber-optic communications cables.[27] According to a recent report by the Office of the Director of National Intelligence: "Deliberate physical attacks on the UCC [undersea cable communications] infrastructure have the potential to significantly disrupt the global economy and degrade national security."[28] The report also notes that coordinated attacks on multiple undersea cables in "a strategic manner could bring a country or region to a standstill."[29] These concerns are not theoretical. On June 11, 2018, the U.S. Department of Treasury imposed sanctions on several Russian entities involved in improving Russia's offensive

---

[24] Nuclear Posture Review, p. 52.

[25] For a greater discussion on the importance of the LRSO. see my article, "Five Myths About a Controversial Nuclear Weapon," *War on the Rocks*, June 20, 2017, https://warontherocks.com/2017/06/five-myths-about-a-controversial-nuclear-weapon/

[26] Nuclear Posture Review, p. 58.

[27] Frank A. Rose, "The Impact of Emerging Security Challenges on Strategic Stability," speech at the University of Virginia, December 2, 2016, https://2009-2017.state.gov/t/avc/rls/264756.htm

[28] Office of the Director of National Intelligence, "Threats to Undersea Cable Communications," September 28, 2017, p. 19, https://www.dni.gov/files/PE/Documents/1---2017-AEP-Threats-to-Undersea-Cable-Communications.pdf.

[29] Ibid

cyber and underwater capabilities. The release states: "Russia has been active in tracking undersea communications cables, which carry the bulk of the world's telecommunications data."[30]

Maintain the cohesion of U.S. alliances

In this increasingly competitive international security environment, America's allies are one of its "asymmetric advantages." The United States' worldwide system of alliances is something that neither Russia nor China possess. And from a military perspective, the United States also needs its allies to effectively deter and defend the U.S. homeland from strategic threats. For example, the upgraded early warning radars in Greenland and the United Kingdom provide early warning against strategic missile attack, track objects in outer space, and directly support the missile defense of the U.S. homeland; the two forward-deployed radars based in Japan support regional and homeland missile defense; and the relay ground stations and other communications around the world directly support U.S. nuclear command and control. Fundamentally, the security of the United States homeland is intricately linked to the security of our allies. Therefore, maintaining the cohesion and effectiveness our alliances must remain the United States' most important foreign policy objective.

Extend the New START Treaty and explore the future role of arms control in managing great power competition

Despite my continuing concerns about Russia's violation of the INF Treaty, I nonetheless believe that the Trump administration should extend New START for an additional five years as allowed by the terms of the treaty, primarily for stability and defense planning reasons. However, I readily acknowledge that it will be politically difficult to extend New START while Russia remains in violation of the INF Treaty.

As the NPR acknowledges, arms control can complement U.S. defense planning. For example, strategic arms control agreements like New START, by bounding the threat and providing transparency and predictability, have enabled U.S. defense planners to design and deploy with confidence an effective deterrent that can survive a first strike by an adversary. And don't take my word for it, here's what General John Hyten, commander of the U.S. Strategic Command, said about New START: "I've stated for the record in the past, and I'll state again, that I'm a — a big supporter [of the treaty]. ... When it comes to nuclear weapons and nuclear capabilities, that bilateral, verifiable arms control agreements are essential to our ability to provide an effective deterrent."[31] Extending New START will also provide time for the United States and Russia to think about what a new framework for U.S.-Russia strategic stability might consist of, especially given further bilateral nuclear reductions appear increasingly unlikely.

---

[30] U.S. Department of the Treasury, "Treasury Sanctions Russian Federal Security Services Enablers," press release, June 11, 2018, https://home.treasury.gov/news/press-releases/sm0410

[31] Steven Young, "New START is a Winner," *All Things Nuclear*, March 16, 2017, https://allthingsnuclear.org/syoung/new-start-is-a-winner

Beyond, New START, we should consider the role future arms control agreements could play in helping manage the return of great power competition in the nuclear sphere. This, however, this will require us to think differently about arms control than we have since the end of the Cold War. Over the past 20 years, nuclear arms control has been primarily focused on reducing the *numbers* of nuclear weapons, and less focused addressing on what strategist Thomas Schelling called the *character of a weapon,* or stability considerations, i.e., limiting the deployment of weapons that were considered destabilizing and could be used in a potential first-strike.

This trend is clearly evident in the decision by the United States to move away from its long-standing arms objective of eliminating "heavy" ICBMs like the Russian SS-18 missile that holds 10 warheads, which we view as highly destabilizing. Land-based MIRVed ICBMs were reduced in the START I Treaty, and ultimately eliminated in START II. However, the United States abandoned this principle in the subsequent Moscow and New START treaties, in large part because we believed that the fundamental political relationship with Russia had changed; therefore, the composition of the Russia strategic forces mattered much less than it previously had. Unfortunately, we were wrong. In this era of renewed great power competition, the priority of any future agreement should be to enhance stability, not necessarily to reduce the number of weapons.

I believe former Secretary of Defense Les Aspin got it right when he stated in 1985: "The whole point of arms control is to take away any incentives to strike first…If we can reduce the numbers of warheads or reduce defense budgets that is frosting on the cake. But the real meat and potatoes of nuclear arms control is to reduce the chance of nuclear war from breaking out."[32]

Engage Russia and China in bilateral stability dialogues

In this area of great power competition, it is vital that the United States maintain open channels of communications with Russia and China, especially in the military-to-military sphere. Therefore, the Trump administration should continue the strategic stability talks that began in 2017. However, these talks should be focused on enhancing deterrence, reducing the risks of miscalculation, and promoting stability -not for the purposes of achieving further nuclear reductions.

With regard to China, the NPR recommends that the United States and China begin a "meaningful dialogue" on nuclear policy, doctrine, and capabilities. This would be a positive step. While China has traditionally been reluctant to engage in a robust government-to-government dialogue on strategic issues, during the last several years of the Obama administration, China did show a willingness to engage more actively in fora such as the U.S.-China Strategic Security Dialogue and the U.S.-China Space Security Talks. The Trump administration should build on this foundation. Recognizing Russia and China's increasing investment in counterspace and offensive cyber capabilities, and the implications of those

---

[32] Peter Ross Range, "Aspin's Ambition," The Washington Post, May 26, 1985,
https://www.washingtonpost.com/archive/lifestyle/magazine/1985/05/26/aspins-ambition/adf67264-d1ef-4536-94d5-76799b5131fe/?utm_term=.35080c06aa56

capabilities on strategic stability, these bilateral dialogues should include a discussion of these and other emerging technology issues.

Advance a broader international conversation about strategic stability

While the United States, Russia, and China have tended the dominate that debate on nuclear weapons and strategic stability issues, other nations, including France, the United Kingdom, India, and Pakistan also impact strategic calculations. For example, Russia has argued any future nuclear arms control discussions must be multilateral, and include all five permanent members (P-5) of the United Nations Security Council. In addition, the nuclear equation in South Asia almost certainly impacts China's calculations.

Therefore, a mechanism should be established to enable a broader discussion on global strategic stability that brings the major players to the table. One place to begin may be in restarting the P-5 process, which was initiated in 2009 to serve as a coordinating mechanism for the P-5 in advance of the 2010 Nonproliferation Treaty (NPT) Review Conference. Through 2015, the P-5 process was primarily focused on advancing arms control and nonproliferation initiatives. In 2015, the members of the group began a broader discussion on nuclear policy and doctrine, resulting in the first P-5 seminar on nuclear policy and doctrine held in New York in October 2016. Surprisingly, all P-5 states found the seminar to be incredibly useful, and agreed to hold additional events. Unfortunately, no additional events have been scheduled since October 2016.

The P-5 process could also be expanded to include states like India and Pakistan at the appropriate time. Indeed, the P-5 has previously met with India and Pakistan in the P-5 + format, focused on finding ways to initiate negotiations on a fissile material cut-off treaty in the Conference on Disarmament.

Develop norms of behavior for emerging domains such as space and cyber

While emerging domains like space and cyber are increasingly impacting stability, we lack effective international norms of behavior to help manage competition. International norms are important for several reasons. First, it's very difficult to identify irresponsible behavior when if you fail to define it. Second, norms can help reduce the risk of miscalculations and accidental conflict between potential adversaries. During the Cold War, the United States and the Soviet Union developed a number of norms such as the 1972 Incidents at Sea Agreement, designed to reduce the risk of accidents between the U.S. and Soviet navies, and the 1988 ICBM/SLBM Launch Notification Agreement, designed to reduce the risk of nuclear war as a result of misinterpretation, miscalculation, or accident.

Developing norms of behavior for emerging domains such as space and cyber could help manage competition between great powers and help mitigate the risk of strategic miscalculation. For example, both the Bush and Obama administration pursued the development of bilateral and multilateral norms of behavior in outer space. And since taking office, senior Trump administration officials have spoken in favor of the need for norms in outer space. In a December 13, 2017 speech at the Eilene Galloway Space Law Symposium, Dr. Scott Pace, executive secretary of the National Space Council stated:

> The Administration seeks to develop non-binding international norms that are complementary to the existing legal regime through both "bottom-up" best practices developed cooperatively with other space actors, and "top-down" non-legally binding confidence-building measures.[33]

Secretary of the Air Force Heather Wilson has also repeatedly expressed support for the development of norms of behavior for outer space.[34] While norms by themselves are not a panacea, they could play an important role in helping manage competition and reduce miscalculations in emerging domains.

Organizing the U.S. government to address great power competition in the strategic domain

Finally, the key point that I've tried to emphasize in my testimony today is the increasing interconnections between the various strategic domains (e.g., nuclear, space, and cyber). This leads to the question of whether the U.S. government is effectively structured to operate in this new and challenging strategic environment, especially at the critically important assistant secretary-level where the vast majority of policy is made. In my opinion, it is not.

The Obama administration got off to a strong start in this area by establishing the Office of the Assistant Secretary of Global Strategic Affairs (ASD/GSA), which brought together under one assistant secretary most of the key strategic capabilities: nuclear forces, missile defense, combating weapons of mass destruction, cyber, and outer space. Unfortunately, this position was eliminated in 2014 for a variety of most bureaucratic reasons. This was a mistake, and I would urge the Trump administration consider reestablishing ASD/GSA or a similar organization at the Department of Defense.

I would also urge the Administration to review whether the State Department is organized effectively to address these cross domain challenges. Responsibility for strategic capabilities are currently resident in a number of functional and regional bureaus within the Department, which in my view, may be an impediment to effective policy implementation.

Conclusion

Mr. Chairman, we have returned to an era of great power competition in which the United States, Russia, and China are competing for the future of the international order. As part of that competition, Russia and China are not only modernizing their nuclear forces, but also developing new and disruptive capabilities such as counterspace and offensive cyber. In this new environment, the United States must find a way to effectively address this challenge in a way that deters potential adversaries, maintains strategic stability, and reduces the risk of nuclear use.

---

[33] Scott Pace, "Space Development, Law, and Values," remarks delivered at the IISL Galloway Space Law Symposium, December 13, 2017.

[34] Scott Maucione, "Air Force has a long to do list for space operations, Wilson says," Federal News Radio, October 5, 2017, https://federalnewsradio.com/air-force/2017/10/air-force-has-long-to-do-list-for-space-operations-wilson-says/

Meeting these goals will require the United States to *complete* the modernization of its strategic nuclear forces; *enhance* the resiliency of its space and cyber infrastructure; *maintain* the cohesion and effectiveness of its alliances; *engage* Russia and China in bilateral dialogues on the future of strategic stability; *pursue* pragmatic arms control initiatives focused enhancing stability and predictability; *begin* a larger international dialogue on global strategic stability that includes a broader set of actors (i.e., the members of the P-5, India, Pakistan); and *develop* norms of responsible behavior for emerging domains such as outer space and cyber.

Mr. POE. I thank all three of you for your testimony and your written statement, and now we will proceed to some questions. You have all the answers. We have some questions for you.

Where did Pakistan get its nuclear capability, Dr. Kim?

Ms. KIM. So I want to note, first of all, that I only work with open source, so there may be greater expertise here on the panel.

Mr. POE. All right, Dr. Long or Mr. Rose, where did Pakistan get its nuclear capability?

Mr. ROSE. Sir, I am not an expert on Pakistan, but I think if you look at the available evidence, there is probably a case that could be made that China potentially helped Pakistan, but I don't know. So again, I am not an expert on Pakistan, but I think that would be a good bet. And you may recall A.Q. Khan played a very, very important role, and there is a possibility of some North Korean links there as well.

Mr. POE. He has been trying to proliferate the whole world, A.Q. Khan.

Do you have any disagreement with what Mr. Rose said, Dr. Long?

Mr. LONG. I don't. I agree with Mr. Rose.

Mr. POE. All right, let me go on to something else. Russia is not in compliance with the INF Treaty. Do any of the three of you disagree with that statement?

Mr. ROSE. No sir.

Mr. POE. Dr. Kim?

Ms. KIM. No.

Mr. POE. And we can agree that in the last year in the NDAA appropriations bill, Congressman Rogers and I introduced legislation to encourage them to be in compliance. Have you seen any change in the Russian endeavor to comply with the INF Treaty?

Dr. Long?

Mr. LONG. I have not. The Russians so far as I am aware continue to deny that they are in violation of the treaty.

Mr. POE. I used to be a judge. The guilty always denied they were guilty, and the more they denied the guilt, the more we knew they were guilty. The Russians are a perfect example of that. I have seen some of their ranting and raving about how they are in compliance and we are not in compliance. That is their position, I understand, but the truth is they are not in compliance. Okay. What are we doing about it?

Mr. ROSE. Sir, I fully agree with your assessment that they are not in compliance. I testified before your subcommittee last year.

Mr. POE. You did.

Mr. ROSE. And I made a number of recommendations. Yes, we should use diplomacy to try to bring them back in. However, the Trump administration has run into the same challenges that the Obama administration found.

Here is what I would say, sir. You have to put the INF violation in a broader context and that broader context is this: Russia does not believe that the Euro-Atlantic architecture put in place at the end of the Cold War is in their interest. And slowly but surely, they have been pulling out all of the building blocks associated with that Euro-Atlantic security architecture.

Mr. POE. Excuse me for interrupting, Mr. Rose. The question is what should we do, not what are they doing.

Mr. ROSE. Yes.

Mr. POE. What should we do?

Mr. ROSE. Well, I would recommend a couple of things. One, moving forward with our strategic modernization program; two——

Mr. POE. And you mean by that ratcheting up our nuclear weapon capability. Is that what you are talking about?

Mr. ROSE. Well, what I would say, sir, is funding our existing program that was laid out. That is really, that is the bedrock of everything we need to do. But then I recommend a couple of other specific things. For example, I think we should develop a conventional variant of the long-range standoff nuclear cruise missile to allow us to hit targets in Russia. I think we should consider some limited cruise missile defense to protect specific assets in Europe. And thirdly, I think we need to work with our allies to make sure that they have precision strike capabilities such as Tomahawk and JASSM-ER.

Mr. POE. All right, one more question about that. We agree that Russia is not in compliance. Is the United States in compliance with the treaty that we signed with the Russians?

Mr. ROSE. Yes sir.

Mr. POE. So we are abiding by the treaty. The Russians are not abiding by the treaty. We know they are not abiding by the treaty, and they are just making matters worse. I mean Putin just recently said that they have new missiles that will be able to take down any of our missiles that we launch. Should we take him seriously when he says that or is he just pontificating?

Dr. Long?

Mr. LONG. He is not pontificating, but a lot of the systems that he has described are in development. They are not fielded systems. So I think you have to take Putin's word seriously but not to imagine that they have a much greater capability than the United States that has been deployed.

Mr. POE. All right, a question about China. China is developing land mass in the South China Sea. It is taking reclaimed areas and making an island in the middle of several places in the South China Sea, then they are militarizing the island claiming that territory for China.

Dr. Kim, what do you think China's long-term plan is for those little military islands that they have started developing in the South China Sea?

Ms. KIM. China wants to expand its control. It wants to expand its military presence, and that is exactly what it is doing.

Mr. POE. So you think they are going to militarize those little islands?

Ms. KIM. They already have begun to do it.

Mr. POE. Yes, some of them.

All right, my time is expired. I will turn to the ranking member from Plymouth, Massachusetts.

Mr. KEATING. Thank you, Mr. Chairman. I want to focus on what our strategy should be in particular, and I want to look at just a few areas if you could comment on it. Number one, with the role of our allies, the strength, and Mr. Rose touched on this, the importance of the role of our allies and the advantages that we have in that regard and what we should be wary of, particularly after our pulling out of the Iran nuclear agreement. Number two, the thing I am most concerned about, I think, is counter space and offensive cyber capabilities, and are we lagging in that way? I have a feeling we are. Should that be a real priority if we have to choose where to focus the most assets?

And the third is the discussion we have. I agree with modernization, but there is also a discussion about a low-yield weapon. To me, once you are in the nuclear theater, you are in, and what sounds like a low-yield kind of weapon, my understanding is that has more destructive powers than Hiroshima. So how low yield, really, is it, and what is our strategic value in that frankly? So could you comment on those three things, anyone? I gave it to you all at once so you could prioritize.

Mr. ROSE. Sir, with regards to the allies, it is our asymmetric advantage from a political perspective, but I want to pound the table on this point. The United States cannot do the Strategic Deterrence Mission or the homeland missile defense mission without access to facilities located on allied territory. So our security is intricately linked to the security of our allies.

Mr. KEATING. Excuse me, what about Turkey? I should mention that specifically.

Mr. ROSE. Turkey. Turkey plays an important role because they host a NATO missile defense radar which provides important radar information to protect all NATO allies including the United States.

Mr. KEATING. Okay, I am sorry. Go ahead.

Mr. ROSE. Yes. With regards to counter space and cyber, I think we are lagging, but I think we are making progress. But I think Congress needs to focus attention on these two areas, and the other area is undersea communications cables. You saw last week that the U.S. Treasury Department sanctioned several Russian entities for concerns that these entities could be going after or tampering with undersea communications cables where 90 percent of all trans-oceanic communications go through. So we have got to focus on those issues as well.

Finally——

Mr. KEATING. Very good. I am glad because that strikes close to home too because two of the areas that will be receiving grants in that area will be SMAST underwater research, University of Massachusetts in my district, and the Woods Hole Institution. So I agree with that too.

Mr. ROSE. And finally on the low-yield system, sir, I mean it is a nuclear weapon. You know, a nuke is a nuke, and we want to try to avoid using nuclear weapons under all circumstances if possible. But at the same time, we need effective capabilities to deter potential——

Mr. KEATING. If I could interrupt, I just want to see if there is anything Dr. Kim or Dr. Long want to focus in on that in particular. But even with the additional revenues we are going to get for funding in these areas, we have to still choose priorities. So I am hearing cyber space, underwater spaces, are things that we should elevate perhaps——

Mr. ROSE. Yes.

Mr. KEATING [continuing]. From where we are.

Dr. Kim?

Ms. KIM. I actually just want to address your point on allies. You know, I think that is our greatest, our alliance system in East Asia is our greatest comparative advantage.

Mr. KEATING. Is Iran, pulling away from that deal do you think that could hurt our ability to——

Ms. KIM. Iran, pulling out of, I mean certainly when our allies are asking us to stay in, I think it is damaging to walk away from a deal that we have committed to. But, you know, turning back to East Asia and the Korean Peninsula, I think it is very important during this time when China is starting to expand its military capabilities and our allies are watching this happen, it is very important that we reassure them that we continue to hold regular military exercises.

Mr. KEATING. Do you favor THAAD, implementation of THAAD in South Korea?

Ms. KIM. You know, the purpose of THAAD is to defend against a North Korean nuclear threat. The threat still exists so in that sense yes, but I think it will be very difficult to sustain an argument for THAAD now that we have signed on to an agreement to pursue a peace regime on the Korean Peninsula.

Mr. KEATING. If I could interrupt.

Dr. Long, just to hear from—thank both of you, yes.

Mr. LONG. Briefly on the question of low-yield nuclear weapons, the United States already fields relatively low-yield systems in the air lag of the triad. The discussion in the Nuclear Posture Review is about expanding that capability to the submarine portion of the triad. It is a relatively inexpensive option if you believe that capability is needed and it improves the odds of delivery. But the utility would depend very much on the circumstances.

Mr. KEATING. And where would you rank that versus, you know, increased counter space and cyber investments?

Mr. LONG. I think in terms of priorities, it is one of the least expensive parts of modernization. So I think counter space and offensive cyber capabilities, and I commend the NDAA last year for calling for a cyber posture review to see what the gaps are. But fundamentally I think the low-yield option is not going to be the big tradeoff with those systems.

Mr. KEATING. Okay. I thank all of you. I yield back.

Mr. POE. I thank the gentleman from Massachusetts. The chair recognizes the gentleman from Illinois, Mr. Schneider.

Mr. SCHNEIDER. Thank you, and thank you to the witnesses for joining us today. And I appreciate the depth of your submitted testimony, and I don't want to focus on all that, but I found it very helpful. Maybe trying to narrow and focus in on a specific region, the Middle East, but I will also include North Korea. Russia and China as well have—it has been reported—have helped Iran, Syria, and North Korea in their nuclear programs.

To what extent do you believe that the two countries have helped these programs with proliferation, and to what extent, if any, are you aware of sanctions on China and Russia for their activities? And I will take it to the next logical conclusion, what should we be doing to address it and prevent it going forward?

Mr. LONG. I will just touch on Russia. Russia has certainly provided support to aspects of Iran's nuclear program including helping build the reactor at Bushehr. I would say the main support Russia has given to Iran has been more in the political sphere and also in the general military arms sphere. So they have sold a variety of systems to Iran. A lot of that was delayed pending the JCPOA but has since gone forward. Russia still believes the JCPOA should be maintained.

Mr. SCHNEIDER. So to the extent, let me just add that Russia now is essentially the linchpin in holding the Assad regime in power. Any evidence of Russia's support for a nuclear program in Syria?

Mr. LONG. As far as I am aware, the support that the Assad regime has received has not been from Russia. It has been more from North Korea, according to open sources.

Mr. SCHNEIDER. All right, Mr. Rose?

Mr. ROSE. Sir, I am not really that competent to respond to that question, but let me get the second part of your question, and that is do we need to work with Russia and China to prevent this proliferation. Absolutely. And that is one of the reasons why I recommended these bilateral strategic stability dialogues. One of the agenda items in those bilateral dialogues needs to be nonproliferation concerns around the world and trying to get them through a bilateral channel to stop any bad behavior.

Mr. SCHNEIDER. Dr. Kim?

Ms. KIM. Yes, so I would just add to that. I think for China in the past, in the second half of the Cold War China did help, for instance, Pakistan with its nuclear weapons program. But having said that, I think in recent years—in recent decades—China hasn't—I don't think it is the central government that has been directly helping countries like North Korea with their nuclear weapons so much as China's lax enforcement of sanctions and export controls.

So that is really where China doesn't live up to its expectations, and I think according to the State Department's compliance report on arms control and nonproliferation, Chinese entities continued to supply missile programs of proliferation concern in 2017. So the concern is still there, and I think it is very important for the United States to work with the central government of Beijing to get them to crack down on these subnational actors who are probably motivated by profit more than strategic concern.

Mr. ROSE. Yes sir. I would agree with Dr. Kim's assessment.

Mr. SCHNEIDER. Great, thank you. Shifting gears a little bit and, you know—the last minute that I have—the long term implications as we are moving down a path with North Korea with nuclear weapons, Iran pursuing nuclear weapons, China, Russia expanding their arsenal—how do we ensure that U.S. strategic interests are preserved and ultimately long term that we are reducing, someday maybe even eliminating, the threat of nuclear war?

Mr. ROSE. Sir, do you mind? What I will say is, one, I think we have to maintain a strong strategic deterrent. But we also—and I talk about this in my testimony—we need to begin a broader discussion on the future of global stability that brings other actors such as India, Pakistan, the U.K, and France into a broader discussion. We do have a process in its infancy through the P5 process, and I recommend in my testimony that we build on that.

Mr. SCHNEIDER. Right.

Dr. Long? Dr. Kim? Anyone have——

Ms. KIM. I would just add that I think the United States needs to set the tone because no one else will in terms of working toward Global Zero. And so I think we should be working to raise the threshold of nuclear conflict not introducing new weapons, and that is something that the United States needs to lead the push for.

Mr. LONG. I would just echo Mr. Rose's comments about the need to maintain a strong strategic deterrent even if that in some cases will seem to lead away from Global Zero at least in the medium term. It is my belief that maintaining that strategic deterrent will be necessary for the foreseeable future.

Mr. SCHNEIDER. Great. Again, thank you for sharing your perspectives, and I am out of time. I yield back.

Mr. POE. We will have another short round of questions. Let's talk about submarines. The United States—and just disregard conventional submarines and talk about nuclear submarines only. My understanding is that the United States has about 14. The Chinese have six—rapidly developing and building more. The Russians have about six—developing rapidly more, the ability to of course take their nuclear weapons with their missiles anywhere they want to in the world.

I have also—it is my understanding—this could be right or wrong, I don't know, but that was also the long-term goal of the North Koreans—to go nuclear, to have nuclear submarines along with nuclear weapons and missiles as well, to develop that for the same reasons because you can move those submarines around.

How are we combating, if we are combating—what are we doing about those facts that Russia and China, primarily, are we able to keep up with what they are developing or not or what is your perspective in that issue—nuclear subs with nuclear weapons on the board?

Dr. Long?

Mr. LONG. So it is true that both Russia and China are working to modernize their strategic nuclear missile submarines. The Russians have deployed a new class. The Chinese are trying to do so as well. The United States plans to deploy a new, more advanced system to replace our Ohio-class submarines—the Columbia-class submarines—so that is part of the nuclear modernization program.

There is also the counter, which is to pursue anti-submarine warfare capabilities which typically have been a competence of the United States Navy—something the Navy is, I think, putting a renewed emphasis on after having spent much of the past 15 years more focused on threats in the Middle East.

Mr. POE. Any other—Mr. Rose?

Mr. ROSE. Sir, I don't have anything more to add than what Dr. Long's——

Mr. POE. Dr. Kim?

Ms. KIM. I don't have anything to add.

Mr. POE. And I want to go back to the South China Sea. What is the United States doing about the South China Sea? When I was over there it didn't seem like we were doing much about patrolling the South China Sea with the Navy. Has that changed any? Do you know, Dr. Kim? What is the United States' policy about keeping the sea lanes open, which I think is what China wants to do, close the South China Sea except with permission of China?

The United States has always been the world leader in keeping the sea lanes open all the way back to the Barbary pirates day. Is that still our policy or not?

Ms. KIM. Yes, it is, sir, and the United States' tool for enforcing that is freedom of navigation patrols, so that is what the United States has been doing. There is a debate about if we need to do more and so, you know.

Mr. POE. Well, do you think we ought to do more?

Ms. KIM. It is hard for me to say at this time, but of course there could be more done. But I would say that I think it is more important to work with our allies so that they are also participating in these patrols so that they are also, you know, claiming or standing up for their claims. And I think it is very important that the United States keeps a neutral position so right now we don't take any sides on who owns what.

Mr. POE. Are you talking about the countries that are affected in the South China Sea?

Ms. KIM. Yes, I am.

Mr. POE. Vietnam is a good example.

Ms. KIM. That is right.

Mr. POE. And others that are concerned about China claiming the South China Sea.

Ms. KIM. Yes. That is correct.

Mr. POE. So you think it is their responsibility to some extent to take care of their own business?

Ms. KIM. Well, I think we should encourage them to stand up for their rights. I think the United States' presence in the area can encourage them to do more and to speak up for their claims and hopefully push all the sides to come to some sort of agreement on what to do about the status of these disputed territories.

Mr. POE. All right, thank you.

Mr. Keating?

Mr. KEATING. I was just going to expand a little bit because we ran out of time on the idea of where to put our priorities and in terms of our nuclear priorities. In terms of the triad in particular, I mean how much—if we are going to look at where we are going, where to invest, where to more maintain our position—where do you think the emphasis should be on land-based weaponry?

Mr. ROSE. Sir, let me say I support the triad. I used to be somewhat skeptical but the more I have learned, very similar to Secretary Mattis. I mean you may have heard that he was initially very skeptical of the long-range standoff weapon and the ground-based strategic deterrent. But as you walk through these issues and you look through the challenges, it becomes more, I think, clear why you need these redundant capabilities.

Mr. KEATING. Okay. But here is what I wanted to focus in on. So yes or no, do you all agree we should maintain all aspects of the triad?

Mr. ROSE. Yes.

Mr. KEATING. Okay, thought so, but now to what extent? If you are looking at the need for cyber space and other areas—you have mentioned underwater threats as greater threats—what level of confidence do we have just saying we have enough on the land based? We can modernize but not expand it—but really concentrate on the others. If you could just, all three, comment on that.

Mr. ROSE. Yes. Sir, though I support the triad, I think we face a challenge with fitting the modernization program into existing budgets. My priorities would be: Number one, the subs; two, B-21 plus the LRSO; and then three, GBSD.

Mr. KEATING. All right, thank you.

Dr. Kim?

Ms. KIM. My technical expertise doesn't extend here so I won't comment.

Mr. KEATING. Okay. Dr. Long?

Mr. LONG. I generally agree with Mr. Rose, but I don't know that I would agree with the prioritization. Part of the challenge is most of these systems have to live for a very long time. We are talking they will outlive probably anyone in this room, and so I think it is hard to say which capabilities will be of greatest utility 70 years from now.

Mr. KEATING. Where can we cut back, if anywhere?

Mr. LONG. I am skeptical there is a lot of room for cutback in the nuclear modernization program. It was a bipartisan agreement that I think, you know, needs to be maintained if for no other rea-son than that it is something that has been agreed to broadly. Both sides of the aisle, I think in both the Obama and Trump adminis-trations, have more or less signed up for this program. I think it—

—

Mr. KEATING. Yes, but you are not elected. So do you have any opinion outside that framework?

Mr. LONG. I think realistically, it is the capabilities we need. I don't see a need for a great expansion of this, but I would be con-cerned about where we would be. I mean most of these programs take so long to field. Now we can talk about acquisition and maybe there are ways to improve that. But given the realities we face, I think it will be tough to say we can do with less of that given that we won't even know what we will get at the end of a program for 10 to 20 years.

Mr. KEATING. Dr. Rose, do you want to comment any further on that?

Mr. ROSE. Well, again, I support the triad. But as I have spoken and written about, I am concerned, you know, when you look at the existing budgets and our other priorities, because in addition to strategic modernization, we have to recapitalize our entire conven-tional force. So it is going to be a challenge. I think what is going to be required is that our elected leaders and the heads of the de-partments, including the Office of Management and Budget, watch this modernization program closely to make sure we are delivering the capabilities on time and on budget.

Mr. KEATING. Yes.

Dr. Long?

Mr. LONG. If I could just add one thing. If there is one area I think should be prioritized—and it is discussed in the Nuclear Posture Review and Mr. Rose has mentioned it—is nuclear command and control. These systems typically are if not neglected at least harder to manage in the aggregate.

Mr. KEATING. Right.

Mr. LONG. They are not a discreet submarine, missile, bomber. They are more dispersed across land, across space, et cetera. So I think that if you are going to place emphasis anywhere, it touches on cyber because you have to make these systems cyber resilient. It touches on space because they extend into space.

Mr. KEATING. You preempted the last question I think I will have time for, and that is the threat of, you know, cyber on our systems. Obviously you prioritize it, so you think it is a great threat.

Dr. Kim? Dr. Rose? Do you want to add to that because clearly we have the greatest system in the world, and if that is threatened, it will be rendered weak.

Mr. ROSE. Sir, I fully agree with that assessment. I was going through Director of National Intelligence Coats' annual threat assessment. Over the last 10 years the number one priority had been terrorism. This year it was cyber threats.

Mr. KEATING. Quite a statement. Okay, I thank all of you again and I yield back.

Mr. POE. I have one more question, sorry. Take these entities— ISIS, Iran, North Korea, China, and Russia. In your opinion, which is the greatest threat to the United States? You just can pick one. Dr. Long?

Mr. LONG. A lot would depend, but I think if you take the viewpoint of the Department of Defense as Secretary Mattis has expressed and Chairman Dunford has expressed, Russia is the only country that can pose an existential threat to the United States. Even China, at least at present, would have a hard time doing that.

Mr. POE. Dr. Kim?

Ms. KIM. I would say our long-term strategic competitor in all domains will be China.

Mr. POE. Thank you.

And Mr. Rose?

Mr. ROSE. I agree with both of them.

Mr. POE. No, you have to break the tie.

Mr. ROSE. That is why. But, you know, let me leave you with this last point. We have multiple threats we need to deal with. That is why we need our allies and strong alliances.

Mr. POE. Right. I thank you all. Thanks again for waiting for us while we were in a series of votes. This concludes the subcommittee, and the subcommittee is adjourned. Thank you very much.

[Whereupon, at 3:14 p.m., the subcommittee was adjourned.]

APPENDIX

SUBCOMMITTEE HEARING NOTICE
COMMITTEE ON FOREIGN AFFAIRS
U.S. HOUSE OF REPRESENTATIVES
WASHINGTON, DC 20515-6128

Subcommittee on Terrorism, Nonproliferation, and Trade
Ted Poe (R-TX), Chairman

TO: MEMBERS OF THE COMMITTEE ON FOREIGN AFFAIRS

You are respectfully requested to attend an OPEN hearing of the Committee on Foreign Affairs to be held by the Subcommittee on Terrorism, Nonproliferation, and Trade in Room 2172 of the Rayburn House Office Building (and available live on the Committee website at http://www.ForeignAffairs.house.gov):

DATE: Thursday, June 21, 2018

TIME: 2:00 p.m.

SUBJECT: Russian and Chinese Nuclear Arsenals: Posture, Proliferation, and the Future of Arms Control

WITNESSES: Austin Long, Ph.D.
Senior Political Scientist
RAND Corporation

Patricia M. Kim, Ph.D.
Stanton Nuclear Security Fellow
Council on Foreign Relations

The Honorable Frank Rose
Senior Fellow
Security and Strategy
Foreign Policy Program
The Brookings Institution
(*Former Assistant Secretary for Arms Control, Verification, and Compliance, U.S. Department of State*)

By Direction of the Chairman

COMMITTEE ON FOREIGN AFFAIRS

MINUTES OF SUBCOMMITTEE ON _______ *Terrorism, Nonproliferation, and Trade* _______ HEARING

Day __*Tuesday*__ Date __*06/21/2018*__ Room _____*2172*_____

Starting Time __*2:28pm*__ Ending Time __*3:14pm*__

Recesses |____| (____to____) (____to____) (____to____) (____to____) (____to____) (____to____)

Presiding Member(s)

Representative Poe

Check all of the following that apply:

Open Session ☑
Executive (closed) Session ☐
Televised ☐

Electronically Recorded (taped) ☑
Stenographic Record ☑

TITLE OF HEARING:

"Russian and Chinese Nuclear Arsenals: Posture, Proliferation, and the Future of Arms Control"

SUBCOMMITTEE MEMBERS PRESENT:

Rep. Poe, Keating, Zeldin, Schneider

NON-SUBCOMMITTEE MEMBERS PRESENT: *(Mark with an * if they are not members of full committee.)*

HEARING WITNESSES: Same as meeting notice attached? Yes ☑ No ☐
(If "no", please list below and include title, agency, department, or organization.)

STATEMENTS FOR THE RECORD: *(List any statements submitted for the record.)*

SFR Submitted by Rep. Poe
SFR Submitted by Rep. Keating

TIME SCHEDULED TO RECONVENE _______
or
TIME ADJOURNED __*3:14pm*__

Subcommittee Staff Associate